The World's Greatest Resumes

The World's Greatest
RESUMES

INTRODUCING THE WORLD'S FIRST RESUME RATER

Robert Wm. Meier

TEN SPEED PRESS
Berkeley/ Toronto

Ten Speed Press
Box 7123
Berkeley, California 94707
www.tenspeed.com

Distributed in Australia by Simon and Schuster Australia, in Canada by Ten Speed Press Canada, in New Zealand by Southern Publishers Group, in South Africa by Real Books, and in the United Kingdom and Europe by Airlift Book Company.

Cover design by Catherine Jacobes
Text design by Jeff Brandenburg

Library of Congress Cataloging-in-Publication Data on file with the publisher.
ISBN 1-58008-677-2

Printed in the United States
First printing, 2005

1 2 3 4 5 6 7 8 9 10 — 09 08 07 06 05

To my wife Marisa, my gift from God,

a woman who is worth much more than rubies or fine gold.

Contents

Part 3 — BEFORE AND AFTER RESUME EXAMPLES

Chapter 4: The Resume Rater in Action

PART I

INTRODUCING THE WORLD'S GREATEST RESUMES

Start Here

CHAPTER ONE
The Resume Quality Rater

CHAPTER TWO
The Resume Quality Rater and RQI

START HERE

You are holding the fruit of thirteen years of labor and over twenty-six thousand hours of career-consulting wisdom. This book teaches a radical departure from the standard resume format that we are all familiar with. Readers who use the techniques will receive enormous benefits by applying the tactics to create a one-of-a-kind resume that allows them to stand out from their job-seeking competition. A word of caution, don't bow to public opinion and *blandize* your story to the vanilla norm that is currently accepted.

How to Change Popular Opinion

To properly introduce new techniques with the least amount of controversy, you need an objective measurement standard that proves the efficacy of the new solution. In other words, without an objective gauge to rate everybody's resume evenly, we are left with individual opinions as our guide to what is excellent. Since opinion is clearly variable, inconsistent, and often unsubstantiated, it was necessary to create a gauge to evaluate (or *evalu-rate*) how well your resume works on today's competitive employment market.

The World's First Resume Rater

This book introduces the world's first resume grader, the Resume Rater, and its attendant index, the Resume Quality Index or RQI. With these tools you can apply the same principles to make your resume excellent that took me, a professional career consultant, thousands and thousands of hours to develop and countless revisions to perfect.

Along with Resume Rater and RQI are dozens of before-and-after examples to help you see how to strengthen your resume content. You can then build an effective resume by measuring the power of your resume, calculating your RQI score to pinpoint weaknesses, and making necessary changes to improve the power score. In other words, you become an expert on the difference between a powerful resume and a weak one, which is part of my plan to help people win jobs they love and attain the financial reward they deserve for their talents.

Essentially, I want to create evangelists on the battlefront of the employment search process who can promote the message that it is possible to improve your job outlook and win the war for a well-paying career.

What's your benefit?

I've heard that headhunters (executive recruiters) are unnecessary if people learn my techniques, because the job seekers could state their value well enough in their resumes that a recruiter would become redundant. I don't know if that is completely true, but I can say that if you learn how to prove your value in your resume, you will largely do what a recruiter does. Yet, you still need access to the recruiter's employer network. So, let's just say that *The World's Greatest Resumes* will help you reveal the characteristics that recruiters look for before they present your qualifications to their corporate clients.

It is said that hiring managers do not want a lot of information. In part that's true, they don't want superfluous data that bore them to death. They do want compelling facts regarding your contributions, which they will use to substantiate their recommendation of you for the job opening. The key is to give them something that they can hang their hat on, something that makes them look like an intelligent appraiser of talent. The Resume Rater will allow you to help these hiring managers because it will force you to look at your resume with the eye of a jeweler to reveal the value that is hidden in the body of your career gem and present this jewel in a way that best illuminates the luster of your capabilities. It is my sincere desire that you increase your earning power and free yourself from a career bottleneck.

Understanding the Book

As far as the way this book was designed, a couple things are worth noting. First, the book is divided into four chapters. Chapter 1 introduces the concept of the Resume Rater. Chapter 2 consists of the Resume Rater questionnaire with its three categories and ten questions. Each Resume Rater is defined in detail in the rule section of the book, chapter 3. Each rule explanation includes two examples of clients that illustrate how I answered the questions. Chapter 4 illustrates the before-and-after resume examples that teach you how to enhance your resume. Finally, the endnote is the proof in the pudding that shows what happened to the client after using the new resume.

How I picked my resume examples

It's important to explain how I picked the examples I use in *The World's Greatest Resumes*. The resumes came from clients who tried to write their own resumes, specifically clients who attempted to write about their most recent jobs. This is important to note since most people don't try to write their most recent role before they hire a resume writer; they figure that's my job. This significantly reduces the resumes I could share. Second, the resumes I chose are from clients who hired me at least twice. That is, they hired me initially to write their resumes and then, typically between three to six years later, came back for a rewrite. What I am trying to point out is that I did not pick only favorites or examples of poorly written resumes so that mine would obviously look better. I picked clients who I could show benefited from the improvement of their presentation using my approach.

At the end of each resume example is a success snapshot summarizing what happened to the client. Here are the details of their success, what areas were fixed, their RQI score, and career statistics. The RQI scores are broken down into intermediary scores according to each of the three categories.

THE RESUME RATER'S THREE CATEGORIES

Category I	PYV—Proving Your Value
Category II	MCG—Proving You Met Corporate Goals
Category III	CPS—Proving Your Career Is Progressing

How to Make This Book Work For You

I guarantee that *The World's Greatest Resumes* will help you write a powerfully compelling resume, which in turn will give you a better chance of achieving your dream job, which in turn will allow you to bloom as a professional, which in turn will be rewarded with better salary, which in turn. . . .

Follow four simple steps as your guide:

1. Grade your resume using the blank grader on page 14.

2. Identify which of the three categories you need to improve.

3. Find resume examples in the book with similar weaknesses as yours and study how I improved their scores.

4. Modify your resume to eliminate your weaknesses.

CHAPTER ONE

If it were not for hope the heart would break.

— Thomas Fuller

THE RESUME QUALITY RATER

Why Is the Resume Rater Necessary?

Anyone who ever started a job search knows the first thing one must do is write a compelling resume. After a little research, one learns there are as many resume writing tactics as there are books on the topic. Amazon alone lists 833 titles under the keyword *resume*. Most of these books are panaceas with the efficacy of snake oil. The problem is, the solutions offered are based on the opinion of authors who may or may not have written many resumes. The beleaguered reader assumes that the accumulated wisdom of a VP of human resources, as one author was prior to becoming a writer, automatically gives him or her the inside track to writing the perfect resume. If that were so, how is it that all these wonderful books make everybody's resume look the same? Or, why is reading a resume as boring as studying the U.S. tax code? Since most opinions are anecdotal rules-of-thumb without valid justification, the job seeker writes a resume that does not prove his or her value or support a hiring decision. The Resume Rater teaches you how to write a compelling resume by creating an objective score and references the areas in your work history that need to be strengthened. It brings objectivity to the resume writing experience and cuts through the chatter of opinion so that job seekers can build a resume that gives them the best opportunity to excel professionally.

Opinions, Opinions, Opinions . . .

We've all heard variations of the following opinions: "Reviewers spend only twenty to thirty seconds reading your resume," or "Don't use an objective statement because it pigeonholes you," or "Don't use the personal pronoun I," or "Put education at the top and references available on request at the bottom," or "Stick to one page," or the opposite, "Two-page resumes make you look successful." These opinions become the mantras by which resumes are written, mantras that can destroy your chance of landing a rewarding job. The crazy need to have someone's opinion validate our resume also leads us to ask a friend, coworker, or parent for input. The problem here is twofold: (1) Your friend probably wrote as many resumes as you have, namely, one, his or her own, and therefore has limited experience to draw from. (2) Your mom or dad is not looking to hire someone with your skills, and hence does not have a vested interest in what you are selling, as does the hiring manager you want to impress. Without a vested interest, mom and dad cannot possibly determine whether your resume defines you as a good fit for the job you are pursuing.

Your resume on the job market is like a snowflake in a blizzard.

When I started writing *The World's Greatest Resumes,* the U.S. Bureau of Labor Statistics noted that fifteen million Americans were unemployed during the previous year. Assuming that typical job seekers send out 250 to 300 resumes during their search, then a massive blizzard of four billion resumes whizzed around the United States as the unemployed sought jobs (the number is probably more like ten billion if you include those who were currently employed but wanted a better situation). What does this mean to you? Without a powerful resume, you have a great chance of becoming a lost snowflake in the resume blizzard.

With the expectation that professionals will change jobs between five and eight times throughout their careers, at an average of four months or more per search, comes the reality that you will spend over two years of your life looking for work. In addition, you will send 1,500 to 3,500 resumes pursuing those openings. At the average of seven jobs pursued with a four-month search each time, professionals earning a $50,000 salary lose $140,000 in wages during their lifetime while finding work. Even with unemployment benefits accounted for, say the max of $1,600 a month, you still lose nearly $100,000. In addition to lost wages is the aggravation, frayed relationships, mental anguish, and loss of self-esteem that attend long job searches. With millions of people spending billions of hours pinning their hopes on an invisible process they barely understand, you can see that it is a good time to bring cohesion and objectivity to the job-search process.

In addition to the resume avalanche conundrum is the fact that the process of finding a job is based largely on blind faith. We send a resume without knowing who receives it, how much time, if any, is spent reading it, or whether a computer is used to review it. Since we typically send fifty times as many resumes as we receive interview opportunities, job seekers remain unclear as to why they are being ignored. What's lacking is critical feedback from potential employers who can help make the resume better. Even if you try to infer from questions asked by hiring managers during the interviews you land, your feedback is skewed because it comes from somebody who appreciated your background enough to call you for the interview. This leads us to modify our resume by whimsy.

What we really need is constructive criticism from somebody who was confused or unimpressed by what we wrote. But we don't receive that type of feedback because people don't call candidates for interviews if they are confused or unimpressed.

The Resume Rater *is* designed to gauge how well your existing resume elevates you above your job-seeking competition. As you follow the principles of the Resume Rater, your resume will read and look radically different than it does right now. But, to be frank, when radical change is introduced as an alternative to a standard format, the problem is to win acceptance in the face of public outcry. In other words, one must overcome resistance to change. More specifically, today's resume formats are typically some variation of the bullet point list or functional format in a chronological order. The resumes that I want you to consider are result oriented, with an emphasis on numbers, percentages, projects, and impacts, defined value rather than implied. This isn't your father's resume.

As I try to change society's view on something as basic as how we sell ourselves on paper, I realize that I'm not the first inventor confronted with overcoming resistance to radical change. Henry Ford had trouble getting the moderately priced Model T accepted as a "horseless carriage" by a general public who was still comfortable with the horse and buggy. However, he persisted until people saw the benefits of the automobile, and now the private car is the standard means of personal travel and Ford Motor Company is part of the Fortune 500. Although it is understandable that some readers will not agree with all of the premises I put forth, I will make every effort to prove that an evolution is needed to improve the outdated process that currently exists in resume design, format, and composition.

Mainstream resume books promote a vanilla norm that causes the least amount of controversy—or positive results

When you consider the resume, the problem is that the experts who form popular opinion, such as human resource executives, directors of university career development centers, newspaper employment editors, headhunters, and resume writers all hold their own beliefs, without a rubric to measure the validity of their assumptions. For you, the job seeker trying to write a great resume, this is cacophony. What rises to mainstream acceptance in many resume books is a vanilla norm that causes the least amount of controversy and criticism. That's why a dot, dot, dot bullet list of duties is what a typical author states as sufficient bait to win an interview. After all, the reasoning goes, it's the interview where details should be elaborated. But I don't believe this is true for a minute. Without the right details given in advance of the interview, you will be overlooked, confuse the reader, and simply not impress him or her enough to pick up the phone and make the call. A great resume sells you before you ever step through the front door of the company's interview room.

Opinion or Science?

The common point that all experts seem to share is they feel their expertise gives them the ability to make valid judgment calls on what makes a powerful resume. You're left guessing which opinion to pick and hoping that you picked the one that works. What you quickly discover when you seek a professional opinion is that the employment editor at the *Chicago Tribune* has her opinion, John Brown the owner of the headhunting firm Brown, Brown & Brown has his opinion, and Robert Meier has his own opinion on how to write a good resume. Multiple opinions on the same subject lead to confusion. The Resume Quality Rater allows you to objectively identify whether you've highlighted your career strengths and minimized your weaknesses—regardless of whose advice you use. It will eliminate the confusing guesswork about which expert opinion to choose by becoming the standard that turns an opinionated process into a measurable science that is capable of correcting bad advice. The idea is to help you write a resume with objective targets to hit so that you improve how well your resume presents your qualifications, which in turn, will reduce your job-search time.

A Sparkling Illustration

The need for an objective system can be illuminated using a simple example. Let's assume you want to buy a diamond engagement ring for your fiancée. Right away you learn that a diamond's quality is appraised on four different categories (the four Cs: cut, color, carat, and clarity). In order to quantify how your diamond stacks up against the competition, you get a GIA (Gemological Institute of America) or AGSL (American Gem Society Laboratories) or

IGI (International Gemological Institute) appraisal of the grade and value of the diamond you want to buy. This is a very wise thing to do when you're spending between $2,000 and $20,000 for a diamond. You do it to protect your investment and make sure that your $10,000 diamond is a sound choice.

Another way to use the ring analogy is to consider what would happen if I wanted to sell you my engagement ring with a diamond center stone. According to my opinion this is a good ring. I like it a lot; I don't see any specks in the diamond, and it sparkles. Now if you were a serious buyer, you would want an objective appraisal stating its value, gold weight, diamond quality, and size. If the appraisal value is $7,500, the potential buyer who offers me $2,800 thinks it's a steal if I sell it to them—not because I said it was worth $7,500, but because the objective standard by which people agree, that is, the IGI appraisal, was a valid gauge of the product's worth. In addition to the four Cs, a GIA report includes data on the shape, cutting style, measurement dimensions, weight, depth, table facet, girdle, culet, finish, clarity, plot, color fluorescence, and additional descriptive comments. Likewise, the resume substantiates an employer's reputation on making good hiring decisions; it supports their investment in your salary, benefits, and associated resources dedicated to your responsibility—which can be millions of dollars.

What if you are a buyer of staff talent, not diamonds? For example, you're a hiring manager of a corporate division. What is the appraisal guide that you use to protect your investment? Of course it's the resume that acts as the primary appraisal guide. A resume is a document stating the approximate value of the employee being considered for the job. An appraisal of a diamond is calculated using current market data, which reflects typical retail prices in addition to the craftsmanship of the item. An appraisal ensures that, in the case of theft or damage, your insurance company will give you an equal replacement value for your item. A resume substantiates the recommendation of the hiring manager, human resource manager, headhunter, or anybody else in the hiring chain. A resume validates their claim that you are worth hiring.

Since objective grading systems are used in so many areas where opinion alone doesn't reveal excellence, it should be obvious that a rating tool to gauge the effectiveness of the resume is long overdue. Objective measurement tools that currently exist in other areas include the following:

EXISTING MEASURING INDICES

- GPA (grade point average): Rates good and bad students
- Batting average: Rates the skill of a baseball player
- IQ (intelligence quotient): Rates the intelligence of a person
- Price/earning ratio: Rates the value of stocks
- Five star quality index: Rates the quality of a hotel

And now, the world's first-ever quality index for resumes:

RQI (Resume Quality Index): Rates the effectiveness of a resume

---

The First Most Important Point in the Book!

The Resume Quality Rater is easy to use, and, once applied to your resume, it will isolate the fluff, that superfluous material that typically makes up over 75 percent of a standard resume, as well as pinpoint which aspects of your work history to highlight. The key to the rater is objectivity. If ten people evaluate the same resume, each should come up with a reasonably close score. If your RQI score is high, 120 to the maximum 135 points, your resume clearly supports why someone should hire you. If your RQI score is below an 80, your resume has not clearly justified a hiring decision, and more important, will probably cause your career search to take longer, eliminate you from good job prospects, and negatively impact your earning potential.

A Word about My Style of Resume Writing

How Much Text is Too Much?

As you read *The World's Greatest Resumes,* hopefully you will see a distinctive quality in my approach relative to the resumes my clients wrote. Although there are obvious differences and subtle differences, the question I'm typically asked is, "Can you write a resume with so much text that it overwhelms the reader and they don't want to read it?" This question is a variation on the old adage "Reviewers read a resume in thirty to sixty seconds." There is some legitimacy in this statement, since reading a resume is work, and reading five hundred resumes is a lot of work. It would appear that making the work easier is better. In part that is true, and in part, this paints only half the picture. If a resume reviewer is only looking for title, company, dates, and education, it's true that it takes thirty seconds to complete an initial scan of a resume to decide keepers from trashers. Since resumes are typically a boring regurgitation of job descriptions, bland recitations of functional tasks, or so confusing that the reviewer gets lost, it is only natural that corporate recruiters look for simple things such as job title, company names, educational pedigrees, and work history continuity. But in any hiring decision, many other factors are relevant in addition to the initial thirty-second scan.

Resumes need substantive content so that you are sold to the company hiring manager or headhunter before the interview. A person's skills are presold by defining his or her impact at each job and then proving the impact had value by defining challenges, strategies, actions, goals, and tactics implemented, as well as, and especially, the results that were achieved. You need a significant amount of the right content to win a hiring decision. Getting recommended for a job means somebody is betting their reputation on you. In addition, hiring new staff is an economic decision. The company is betting scarce resources on your salary, benefits, and the capital budget you will manage. If I bet my reputation and my company's scarce resources on you, I'd better read how you impacted your previous company's bottom line in a definitive, detailed manner. Ironically, I have many clients with three-, four-, and five-page resumes that I convert into one- and two-page resumes. Although in a good resume, content is king, the fact is that content needs to be startlingly impressive to justify its presence in the scarce resource that an 8.5 x 11-inch sheet of paper represents. So, I provide only data that sell you, not irrelevant information that describes your daily duties.

Resumes written only to pass a thirty-second initial review limit your chance of winning the interview.

To contrast the two types of reviews your resume must pass, the initial thirty-second review and the final hire review, consider a recent client's situation. John had worked at four telecommunication companies: Cimco, Mavrix, Focal, and Ameritech (now SBC) over a thirty-year span. If I'd written his resume to pass only the thirty-second review, he could have easily been considered too old and outdated to win the job offer. My goal was to help the initial resume reviewer recommend my client to his or her boss, typically a senior manager in the hiring chain. The senior hiring manager needs a resume that can jump the final-hire screening hurdle, which lasts a lot longer than thirty seconds. John's old dot, dot, dot resume (bullet point list of duties) did not prove his contributions compellingly enough to help an initial reviewer make a positive recommendation. Bullet-list resumes are usually so drab and boring that reviewers typically look only at job titles, length of work history, and education. If a resume doesn't have the content to prove the value of your contributions you can be eliminated by a peer with a better pedigree. Since my client is over fifty years old, the boss could look at his resume and note that John was not a college graduate and had been in the military as far back as 1969. He could ask questions like, "How old is this guy?" Instead of, "Wow, I can't believe he increased Cimco's revenues 20 percent in a single year." If his value doesn't far surpass his handicaps, the senior manager may think, "Can't we get some young guy that is happy making fifty grand a year?" In the end, he might veto the hire, embarrass the initial reviewer, and kill John's chance of winning the job offer.

Write a Resume with Content That Deserves to Be Read

Another way to look at the question on amount of content is the reverse. If I'm the hiring manager and I'm *not* looking for someone with your background, then you can't write few enough words. If you're a good fit for the job opening and your resume states the challenges you met and your contributions to the company and highlights key projects that prove your value, then the hiring manager has a tool to defend his or her recommendation. A manager will spend time learning who you are in order to make a good hiring decision, especially if he or she is risking his reputation on the recommendation. He or she will spend more than thirty seconds reviewing your credentials. My resumes are text intensive, yet very effective, as my clients' success stories prove.

CHAPTER TWO

God gives, but man must open his hand.

— German Proverb

THE RESUME QUALITY RATER AND RQI

Understanding the Three Categories and Scoring Section

Welcome to the Resume Quality Rater and Resume Quality Index

The grading system is broken into ten questions spread across three categories:

Category 1   Your resume must prove the value of your results numerically.

Category 2   Your resume must prove you met corporate goals.

Category 3   Your resume must prove your career is progressing, not flat or declining.

The first and second categories are where the most points are earned, up to fifteen points per question. The third category is important but at a slightly lower level, a maximum of ten points each. The grading system tops out at 135 points. Each question has three possible responses: "yes," "no," and "some." For all of the questions except number two, a yes answer gives you the most points (fifteen or ten each), a no answer gives you zero (0) points, and a some answer always awards five points (5). The second question reverses this and awards fifteen points for a no answer, zero points for a yes, and five for a some answer (refer to the key below). The sum of the point total is your RQI score. The higher the score the more powerful your resume is at distinguishing you as exceptional and worth interviewing.

At the bottom of each Resume Rater is the score box and grading key that states how much a poor score lengthens a job search. It is important to teach the reader that there are actual consequences for bad scores, that is, poor quality resumes. My rationale for the one-week-per-ten-points ratio is simply taken from my observation as a career coach to four thousand clients over the past thirteen years. Whether one or two weeks per ten points is valid is arguable, but I feel this is a fair and conservative estimation.

The next few pages introduces each of the four sections independently so as to isolate what each category is trying to reveal in your background.

The Resume Quality Rater

How Hot Is Your Resume? — Score Its Effectiveness

I. Does Your Resume . . . Prove Your Value

	YES	NO	SOME
1. Define contributions using numbers, percentages, and statistics.	Y	N	S
2. Define functional tasks rather than results.	Y	N	S
3. Clearly support your results with evidence.	Y	N	S
4. Identify largest, first ever, top 20 percent performance results.	Y	N	S
5. Prove you helped reduce costs, earn money, or add value in your company.	Y	N	S

II. Does Your Resume . . . Prove You Met Corporate Goals

	YES	NO	SOME
6. Define the projects you led or supported and explain the results.	Y	N	S
7. Explain corporate goals and how you helped meet those goals.	Y	N	S

III. Does Your Resume . . . Prove Your Career Is Progressing

	YES	NO	SOME
8. Define how each job progressed in challenge and responsibility.	Y	N	S
9. Prove current job skills correlate to your career objective.	Y	N	S
10. Show progressive titles, advanced education, and good corporate pedigree.	Y	N	S

The Resume Rater Scoring Key

Question	Points for Each Answer			Y (Yes)	N (No)	S (Some)
1.	Y = 15	N = 0	S = 5			
2.	Y = 0	N = 15	S = 5			
3.	Y = 15	N = 0	S = 5			
4.	Y = 15	N = 0	S = 5			
5.	Y = 15	N = 0	S = 5			
6.	Y = 15	N = 0	S = 5			
7.	Y = 15	N = 0	S = 5			
8.	Y = 10	N = 0	S = 5			
9.	Y = 10	N = 0	S = 5			
10.	Y = 10	N = 0	S = 5			
Sum Total = RQI Score:						

Scoring: Each 10 points below a virtuous resume score of 120 points adds one to two weeks of search time to your job hunt (this is added on top of the standard length of one month per $10,000 in base salary you expect to earn).

Example: Your score = __x__ (120- __x__ = __y__)
You scored __y__ points below 120

Problem: You're adding y×.1 to y×.2 weeks to your job search

Score _____ / your resume has:

120–135	=	**Power Pro**
100–121	=	**Power Prospect**
85–101	=	**Power Pansy**
Under 85	=	**Power Puff**

Section I: Prove Your Value (PYV)

To win a job offer, the name of the game is proving value. Section one of the Resume Rater is where you prove your value. Professionals either win or lose the battle for positive perception by how well they write information that convinces the hiring authority they are worth their salary. If you don't explicitly define your contribution in quantifiable results that are substantiated with strategies, challenges, tactics, and actions, then you kill your chance of wowing the employer. It is important to write your resume so they are truly impressed with the scope of your accomplishments, the critical nature of the expectations you met, and how you attained your results. I call this a WOW resume style.

Unfortunately, most people don't write their resumes believing they have to prove anything on paper, so their results are tepid or, worse yet, confusing. Hence, they often zero out in this section. That's too bad, because when I meet with a client I usually uncover numerous contributions they made that can be measured quantitatively. It just takes creativity to calculate the numbers and conservative estimations or comparisons to their peers in order to properly illustrate their importance.

- Question one scales your accomplishments in a framework where anyone can see your value.

- Question two is a trick question. Nobody wants to read a job description. If you answered yes, you probably listed job tasks or functional data rather than results.

- Question three challenges us to validate our claims with corroborating evidence.

- Question four separates you from the pack. It is a type of the 80/20 rule (i.e., "Top 20%" employees usually accomplish "largest" or "first-ever" feats).

- Question five focuses on the bottom-line financial impact of your involvement.

The five questions are worth a maximum of fifteen points each. All Yes answers give you fifteen points except the second question, where a No is worth fifteen. Any Some answers are worth five points. The entire PYV (Prove Your Value) section is worth a total of 75 points.

I. Does Your Resume . . . Prove Your Value	YES	NO	SOME
1. Define contributions using numbers, percentages, and statistics.	Y	N	S
2. Define functional tasks rather than results.	Y	N	S
3. Clearly support your results with evidence.	Y	N	S
4. Identify largest, first ever, top 20% performance results.	Y	N	S
5. Prove you helped reduce costs, earn money, or add value in your company.	Y	N	S

This category truly allows you to shine. The dynamic goals that define a company and the staff they use to meet those goals are the ones that sparkle like diamonds among baubles.

This is a difficult section for us to succeed in without a significant amount of creative forethought. We have to think differently. Don't simply list points that outline job duties. You must communicate, in the body of the resume, the goal of the project, the challenges, the expectations, and the results as they impacted the company. We also have to do this concisely and compellingly. The special key to writing about projects you've supported is to blurt out the entire project scope, then whittle it down to three or four lines of text with category titles to lead the reader's eye.

Section II: Prove You Met Corporate Goals (MCG)

If you properly define how you contributed to the corporate goals of a your present or past employer, you prove you absorbed their mission and are a team player with the vision to support the objectives of another company. If you can't prove you met corporate goals, you reduce your value to that of a task-oriented functionary. Task-oriented professionals don't get promoted and rarely find rewarding work.

- Question six allows you to outline the projects you've supported, your role in them, and the successful outcome relative to expectations.

- Question seven uncovers dynamic inflections or corporate transitions, business process improvements, new ventures, or anything in which the company engaged your efforts to improve their bottom line.

With only two questions, the MCG category (Met Corporate Goals) is worth a total of thirty points, fifteen for each yes answer, five for each some answer, and zero for a no answer.

II. Does Your Resume . . . Prove You Met Corporate Goals	YES	NO	SOME
6. Define the projects you led or supported and explain the results.	Y	N	S
7. Explain corporate goals and how you helped meet those goals.	Y	N	S

Section III: Prove Your Career Is Progressing

These last three questions prove to the hiring manager that you are an employee who is progressing as a professional. In other words, you're peaking and can handle increasingly difficult responsibilities without a problem. This section has the fewest points possible for each question (ten rather than fifteen for a yes answer). The points are reduced because I believe that companies want producers more than anything else, and this section doesn't so much reveal producers as it does reveal good professional pedigree. A good pedigree recognizes, for example, that IBM has a better reputation for hiring talent than does a lesser-known company, such as Suzy's Donut Hut, so those with a Fortune 500 work history earn credit here (see question number ten). Nevertheless, if you worked at IBM and accomplished nothing you will have a harder time finding fulfilling work than someone who worked for Suzy's Donut Hut and increased patron loyalty and thus added $1,000,000 in revenues annually. Yet the IBM name does have a cachet that is worth noting and worth a few points.

- Question eight simply illustrates how you are ready to take the next step in your career progress.

- Question nine correlates how your skills match the recruiter's needs.

- Question ten refers to a career path you do or do not already possess.

Questions eight and ten are important to answer in a way that illustrates how you are growing as a professional. Nobody wants to hire "dead wood" or someone who is not attempting to better themselves, extend their capabilities, or take risks.

The total points possible in the career progress section are thirty, ten for each yes answer and zero for a no. Finally, a some answer is worth five points.

III. Does Your Resume . . . Prove Your Career Is Progressing

	YES	NO	SOME
8. Define how each job progressed in challenge and responsibility.	Y	N	S
9. Prove current job skills correlate to your career objective.	Y	N	S
10. Show progressive titles, advanced education, and good corporate pedigree.	Y	N	S

Scoring

This is a fairly self-explanatory section with two elements. The first part is where your score is calculated and then referenced to what happens to your career search length—the lower your score, the longer the search length. This simply means that bad resumes are overlooked and lengthen career searches. As a rule of thumb, for each ten points below the Power Pro Score of 120 to 135, you will need to search a week longer for employment. On the other hand, a great score, 120 points or above, takes time off a career search by a corresponding amount. The total is your RQI score—Resume Quality Index.

The four power categories, Pro/Prospect/Pansy/Puff, relate to the combined points of the three categories. The higher the score, the better your prospect of standing out among other job seekers as the obvious choice and most likely candidate to be picked for an interview.

Scoring: Each 10 points below a virtuous resume score of 120 points adds one to two weeks of search time to your job hunt (this is added on top of the standard length of one month per $10,000 in base salary you expect to earn).

Example: Your score = _x_ (120- _x_ = _y_)
You scored _y_ points below 120

Problem: You're adding _y_ to _2y_ weeks to your job search

Score _____ / your resume has:		
120–136	=	**Power Pro**
100–121	=	**Power Prospect**
85–101	=	**Power Pansy**
Under 85	=	**Power Puff**

PART 2

THE 10 RULES OF A POWERFUL RESUME

Resume Quality Rater's
Ten Questions Defined

A wise man will make more opportunities than he finds.

— Francis Bacon

RESUME QUALITY RATER'S TEN QUESTIONS DEFINED

RESUME QUALITY RATER RULE 1

Numbers, Percentages, and Quantities (NPQs) Define Your Contributions Numerically

Like a culinary chef adding the perfect spice to create a delicate sauce, a great resume has the right balance of numbers, percentages, and quantities to wow the hiring manager. In cooking, a calibrated blend of ingredients highlight certain flavor notes. Likewise, using the right numbers will clarify the impact you made at your previous jobs and focus the reader's attention on what sells you. But, at the risk of stretching the analogy too far, like novice cooks who fear using cayenne pepper because it may offend sensitive palettes, most people are afraid of using NPQs because they think it's better to be safe and bland rather than use numbers that can stir controversy. Really, NPQs for most professionals are just too hot to handle. Don't allow yourself to give up so easily. Just because you struggle to decide how to calculate your statistics doesn't justify their omission. You need to push yourself to take a blank piece of paper and make educated guesses. That's what I do for my clients, and you'd be surprised how accurate these guesses are. People believe that their bottom line contribution may not impress. Or they think that without documentation to substantiate their claims, the reader may not believe the results. Other professionals simply can't remember, so why push themselves to recall, "I'll be general, they'll get the gist of my value." Baloney!

No excuses, you can't leave out Numbers, Percentages, and Quantities
NPQs are the only way to give the reader's mind the framework to fully understand the impact of your accomplishments. Unless you quantify your contributions, your value is only implied, and implied value is hidden, and hidden value is no value. So don't be afraid to use NPQs wholeheartedly.

When it comes to people using NPQs, two camps exist. On one extreme, job seekers avoid NPQs like the plague and blur their impact with vague statements such as "significantly increased returns" rather than "enhanced ROI by 300% or $50 million in two years." On the other hand, you have people who sprinkle NPQs liberally in their resume but fail to support them with enough information for validation, so credibility is lost. They argue that interviewers cannot possibly confirm or deny their numbers, so any positive figures will work. The problem with using unsubstantiated NPQs is you risk irritating the reviewer, raising flags that make them skeptical, and, quite likely, very confused.

The correct balance is to use numbers regularly, but err on the side of modesty and support the numbers you use with evidence of how you achieved them. If you can't remember exact figures, as few can, use statements such as "up to" or "peak values" that you can remember. It is OK to make educated guesses to calculate your worth. It may be impossible to be 100 percent precise, since we rarely have financial reports to verify the statistics, but it *is* critical to be honest so that you can look the interviewer in the eye when you explain your numbers. Ultimately, *you* must be convinced that you are being accurate.

NPQ Illustration

Here's an illustration I use with new clients to support the need for NPQs. What if I said to you, "I have a lot of money in the top drawer of my desk"? A "lot" implies something. You might think that I have $50 in my drawer, or you might guess $500. Either way, you are only speculating as to what a "lot" means to you. Unless I open up the drawer and show you $50,000 stacked neatly, a "lot" can mean anything, or nothing at all. If you keep the drawer shut on your personal value, your value remains invisible. Open up the drawer and enumerate how you added value to your company and nobody will be left wondering what you have done to justify your salary.

NPQ Questions

To use NPQs correctly, ask yourself intelligent questions regarding anything you can possibly think of that helped your company. For example:

How did I contribute in my job to improve revenues, streamline operations, enhance efficiencies, reduce costs, improve speed of product delivery, or simplify processes?

A numerical scale frames the mind's eye to visualize how your results truly impacted the company and added value. Without a framework, you drop the reader into a picture where they easily get lost. If you cannot scale your value numerically, people are not able to visualize how the company that hired you benefited from your employment.

Building Credibility

The best way to use numbers, percentages, and quantities is in a manner that supports your professional credibility. Good numbers build reader excitement and elevates their appreciation. It does you no good to force a number on the reader without adding the proper context. As an illustration, think of how a great movie director uses a back story to explain the history of the movie's plotline to help the audience understand what is about to happen, and more important, what they should care about. Likewise you need to write enough back story about the challenges you met or problems you solved so that your numbers build reader excitement and appreciation. Without a good back story, you confuse the reader. It's like telling the punch line of a joke. Without foundation, the punch line loses its punch. In your resume you need to ensure that when you get to your successes, you note enough of the corporate expectations, projections, and forecasts relative to your accomplishments that the reader gets the full picture and appreciates your contribution.

EXAMPLE 1

His Resume Stated . . .

1986–1996 Gem Creations, Inc. Jewelry Remount
1992–1996 Executive VP

Managed sales, operations, and marketing. Directed up to 150 sales and marketing staff, including administrative support specialists and 35 two-member teams consisting of a sales representative and a jeweler, providing in-store sales and remount services for consumers at over 2,000 retailer outlets in North America. Supervised all merchandising and promotion at retailers of fine jewelry to bring consumers to their stores for custom-design remounts.

My Rewrite Stated . . .

Overview	Directed a team of 150 sales, operations, and administrative staff.	
Goal #1	*Cut Cost*	Optimized 35 sales teams (consisting of a sales rep and a jeweler) who conducted 8,500–10,000 jewelry-remount shows per year at 2,000 jewelry stores in North America.
	Action	Created the first-ever ***Master Schedule,*** an extremely efficient tracking tool that calculated and optimized team travel time to minimize excessive downtime.
	Result	The master schedule reduced per show costs an average of $750 to $500, thereby ***saving $2.5MM.***

The Key—Replaced a bland description of duties that fail to explain his impact and hides his value.

Change—Minimized his job description and went directly to his greatest impact to define how he saved Gem Creations $2.5 million.

EXAMPLE 2

Her Resume Stated . . .

1982–1993 Teacher of Video Production—University of Oxford, Oxford, England
Supervising and teaching 2nd and 3rd year university students the various skills required in order to complete a successful video project. This instruction included topics on scripting, filming, directing, use of three-color camera studio, and editing, along with a very pronounced pastoral role.

My Rewrite Stated . . .

1982–1993 *Assistant Professor,* **UNIVERSITY OF OXFORD, Oxford, England**
Taught honor's *Video Production* courses to undergraduate students. Covered: scripting, directing, using three-color camera studio, lighting, mixing, and editing.

Project   Created the university's International Recruitment Promotional Video, a 47-minute video targeting the Asian Market.

Result   Foreign enrollment increased from 2% to 22% over 10 years, representing 2,400 new students and **$28MM** in tuition revenues.

The Key—All the client said about her job was a bland recitation of the job description.

Change—After writing a specific description of key job functions, I focused on how she helped her school grow their tuition base by $28 million.

RESUME QUALITY RATER RULE 2

Don't Describe Job Tasks

Remember, question two is somewhat of a trick question. Since all nine other questions give you the most points for a yes, it is tempting to think that describing job tasks is beneficial, but that is not the case here. Don't write your resume with the tasks or functions you handled in mind. Think instead of the challenges you've met, the tactics you executed, and the strategies you implemented. The key is to give the reader the results that were derived from meeting those challenges, executing those tactics, and taking those action steps. If you explain the needs that you were meeting, the challenges you were overcoming, and the mandates you were expected to address, then your results will have greater impact.

Approximately 95 percent of my clients write their resumes in a manner that is task or functionally focused. They write their resumes like a job description. For example, many people will write, "Responsible for home sales and marketing research exposure. Responsible for monitoring progress of business plan performance. Responsible for traveling to each operating unit to analyze current business. Responsible for developing realistic and actionable business plans. Responsible for identifying new product needs." People who communicate task or functional data fail to realize that most people couldn't care less. It's not the task that creates the WOW for the person reviewing your resume, or that illuminates your genius, or elevates you above your competition. Rest assured that any sentence in your resume that begins with the phrase "*responsible for* . . ." is focusing on task or functional information, not on how you added value.

Use These Keys

To improve the readability of your resume, always think you've done something marvelous, something genius, something brilliant, something amazing. I always believe that my client's contribution is extraordinary. It's my job to prove that I'm right. Everything I do when I interview my clients is to find the "wow" or "gee-whiz" elements in their careers. If you take the perspective that what you've done is marvelous and you set out to prove it, you have a better chance of accomplishing that goal than if you set out to merely communicate your duties and responsibilities.

Another reason I think people fail to write a compelling resume is they don't see that writing combines art with science. They err on the science side and treat the resume like a formula. That's why resumes often look similar: name at the top, address next, objective statement, some with summaries, some not, education, experience, responsible for . . . dot-dot-dot. They fail to think of their careers like a raw jewel or a block of marble to sculpt. If you're a jeweler, your art is cutting an exquisite gem out of the raw material. It's not unusual for me, after having written four thousand resumes, to spend ten to twenty hours composing a resume. When I write, I chip, chip, chip at the diamond of my client's career, so that what's finally left is the distilled essence, the "wow," the "gee-whiz" of their accomplishments.

EXAMPLE 1

His Resume Stated . . .

1985–Present   **CHIEF ENGINEER 400 East Wacker Drive, Chicago, IL**
Responsible for day-to-day operations of a commercial landmark building with 41 floors erected in 1928 alongside the Chicago River in the key business district. Oversee operation and maintenance of three boilers, evaporative cooling towers, screw machines, VAV ventilating system, domestic water systems, and five gearless elevators. Supervise 11 custodians and security staff as well as buildouts and subcontractors. Maintain code compliance for large, first-floor restaurant. Survived three turnovers in management.

My Rewrite Stated . . .

1985–2003 *Chief Engineer,* **Compass Management & Leasing, Chicago, IL**
Manage a 41-floor, multitenant commercial landmark building. Oversee annual budgets, leasing issues, and vendor contracts. Supervise 11 custodians and security staff. Act as building contractor during buildout/rehabs.

Project 1   **EXTERIOR RESTORATION:** Oversaw a **$2.5MM** masonry project involving 6 contractors and 35 workers that impacted 70% of the building's exterior.

> *Focus*   Justified expenditures for each phase, monitored contractors to ensure contract compliance, and suggested alternatives to reduce expense.

> *Result*   Directed the architectural engineering firm to implement a modular scaffolding system that saved $160K.

Project 2   **TENANT BUILDOUTS:** Managed 150 tenant projects over 12 years costing $12MM.

Focus   Developed 18 subcontractor relationships, i.e., mill workers, lighting, HVAC, carpet, electrical, and data station installers.

Result   Earned $600,000 in revenues from the 5% project fee that tenants paid.

The Key—He only listed daily operational duties.

Change—After a brief job description, I highlighted two projects that proved he added value to his company in money saved and money earned.

─────────────────── **EXAMPLE 2** ───────────────────

His Resume Stated . . .

Experience
> **Sound Designer**
> **Sony Games**
> **April 1995–Current (Full-Time)**
> Responsible for video game sound playback engine designing and producing audio content that included sound FX designing and BGM scoring.

My Rewrite Stated . . .

4/95–9/00   *Product Designer*, **SONY GAMES**

Overview...   Developed multimedia products distributed globally for a billion dollar Japanese computer entertainment enterprise. My products sold primarily in the United States, which in 1995 represented 20% of Sony's revenues and grew to 35% by 2000 (Europe = 10%; Asia = 50%).

Challenge 1   I'm Chinese working for a Japanese company making video games for a U.S. market where the audience demands perfect idiomatic assimilation to U.S. slang and cultural meaning.

Challenge 2   Creating product for Midway, as well as Sony PlayStation, Sega Dreamcast, and Nintendo platforms.

Actions   Localized Japanese entertainment products for the U.S. culture, including
- *The Simpsons Go Bowling*
- NBA's *In The Zone*
- *Metal Gear* (world's #1 selling PlayStation game)

Impact   My 19 products have generated $300MM in total revenues.

> *The Key*—His explanation was full of technical jargon and lacked impact.
>
> *Change*—In this resume, I illustrated how complicated it is to develop international computer games. I also matched his goal of finding a U.S. company needing a Chinese ex-pat to launch products in China.

RESUME QUALITY RATER RULE 3

Prove Your Results

Evidence overcomes the hiring manager's disbelief and skepticism as to the veracity of your resume. It is widely assumed that most resumes have errors or outright lies. According to an article written by Wayne Tompkins in The (Louisville, Ky.) *Courier-Journal,* September 2000, a company called the Careershop conducted a three-month, anonymous online survey and found that 73 percent of nearly seven hundred people who responded admitted to lying on their resumes. Whether intentional or accidental, this leads many reviewers to dismiss anything they feel has exaggeration, and once you lose the game of building credibility, you're taken out of the picture.

Hiring managers reject ninety-nine out of a hundred job candidates, so the very process of seeking new staff turns hiring managers into skeptics.

For the hiring company, a new hire is always an economic decision—assuming you're not planning to work for free. You're going to expect a salary and benefits package, so somebody has to decide whether it's worth it to their company to choose you from the competition. They're basing the decision on the bet that you will bring substantially more value to the company than they pay you. In other words, the critical areas they'll be examining are whether your contribution will justify the expense. If you don't prove you can deliver results, it is nearly impossible for a hiring manager to bet his or her reputation on making a positive hiring recommendation on you.

Make the Implicit Explicit

Proving results is critical to support the idea that you are an exceptional performer. It's one thing to tell people your accomplishments and another to prove them. I would say that most people score a zero on this question because they don't even try to define a result in the first place (at least 80 percent of my clients never try to prove anything in their resumes). The few clients who do put in some sort of result or accomplishment think very little of the need to substantiate their statistics. Proving results takes forethought. For example, a client of mine, realizing he needed to define his impact, wrote: "Product developed and launched in record time earned total revenues of $106 million and projected margin of 45 percent in six months." Amazing statistics, but the problem for my client is no one believed him, since he didn't back up his results with how he accomplished them. For the person reviewing your resume, his or her entire perspective is to be skeptical and disbelieving.

What You're up Against

For each job opening a hiring manager receives over two hundred resumes, of which he may call ten for a phone screening. Out of these ten finalists he will probably pick two or three for a face-to-face interview, from which, he will make one job offer. What are corporate recruiters doing 99 percent of the time? They are screening and eliminating candidates. The only thing most hiring managers need is one excuse to determine you don't fit their search profile. If they don't believe your results because you don't support them with enough background information to make your results believable, you are eliminated. When somebody quotes incredibly amazing statistics, facts, numbers, and results without properly supporting the statistics with strategies, tactics, and action steps, these results, instead of illuminating the candidates' capabilities, cause interviewers to be suspicious, roll their eyes, and dismiss them as embellishers (a euphemism for liars).

Don't Buy the Lie

The argument I am confronted with quite regularly is that people think that the only staff who have a direct impact on making money for the company are senior executives, salespeople, and managers with profit/loss (P&L) responsibilities. So teachers, social workers, nurses, secretaries, customer service reps, military members, and institutional administrators at a hospital, university, or the government don't need to show their impact on the bottom line. The truth is that if you prove that your contribution made something more effective, efficient, saved time, produced twice as much work with half as many people, or gained better results for the same number of work hours, then you are saving money. Other things you can say that impacted the bottom line include implementing new programs, reaching a broader consumer base, or enhancing customer service. Look closely at the examples included in this book, and you will see that there are as many ways for a professional to contribute as there are ways to calculate that contribution.

-------------------------------- **EXAMPLE 1** --------------------------------

His Resume Stated . . .

General Manager, Chicago Northwestern R.R.
• Increased revenue from $36 million to $79 million in 15 years.

My Rewrite stated . . .

1986–1/02   *General Manager,* **CHICAGO NORTHWESTERN RAILROAD**
Overview   Managed a $78M railroad operation with 800 staff who serve 200 corporate clients.

Challenge   **REDIRECT NORTHWESTERN TO PROFITABILITY**—this railroad had experienced severely declining revenues (they fell 23% by 1986 when I became GM), the cumulative drop lost $55M from peak revenues in 1981.

Actions		Introduced business development, organizational, and cost-management initiatives to capture new revenues and enhance efficiencies.
Results	*Dividends*	Paid $27M in dividends, 1987–2001. These were the first dividends paid in 27 years.
	Equity	Increased stockholders' equity 300%.
	Revenue	Grew 125% in 15 years ($36M to $79M).

The Key—His wonderful result completely lacked support.

Change—Although it may take more words to support your contribution, if you accomplish something significant (like growing revenues by $43 million), a hiring manager will read the data.

EXAMPLE 2

His Resume Stated . . .

Marketing Manager BELCO COMMUNICATIONS, INC.
- Developed strategy and implemented team to sell, market, promote, and support data services to business generating $24 million of yearly revenue

My Rewrite Stated . . .

1998–2000	**Marketing Manager**	**BELCO COMMUNICATIONS, INC.**

My Mandate from the Executive Team:
- Launch DSL & Data Products to complement existing voice business.
- Leverage Belco's 40% excess network capacity and support the IPO.

Strategies
1. Authored the business case as our launch blueprint.
2. Full P&L role to develop all life-cycle elements of the products.
3. Enhanced success elements from existing programs with a 4-step production plan.

Benefit to Belco
- DSL and Data Products add $24M annually.
- Belco launched a successful IPO on 7/99 that generated $130M.

The Key—My client explained how he built a new $24M business segment in one bullet point.

Change—To substantiate his claims I defined the strategies he implemented and the benefit to his company because of his involvement.

RESUME QUALITY RATER RULE 4

Identify Largest, First-Ever, Top 20 Percent Results

To introduce this point, I need to explain that most hiring managers only look for top performers and fast-trackers (that is, if they are hiring managers who are secure in their roles and not afraid of someone trying to take their job). Hiring managers want to think they are hiring the best, so the fourth point attempts to elevate your profile to the top of the candidate pool. The best way to understand this point is to refer to the famous 80/20 rule, which was initially coined by Wilfredo Pareto (a turn-of-the-century Italian economist). According to his presupposition, which has permeated into many common areas, only 20 percent of a company's best employees produce 80 percent of the value. So in a ten-person sales staff, the top two account executives will win clients who produce 80 percent of the sales. Whether this is true or not, most businesses hire staff according to this rule. In other words, they seek those rare and exceptional performers who can make a difference. The trick for hiring managers is to identify these top performers, and you want to give them every chance to see that you're that person.

When we first graduate from college, the crudest form of measurement for top performers is the GPA. Although many companies realize that book smarts don't always correlate with employee effectiveness, a company typically believes that new hires are less likely to fail if they drove themselves to excel academically. Sometimes it's not even personal accomplishments that guide the recruiter, but the credibility conveyed by the academic institution itself. That's why Ivy League schools have a less difficult time getting their students employed than non-Ivy League schools. The assumption in the employment market is that the Ivy League makes it so difficult to be enrolled in the first place that an Ivy League graduate should be considered a top performer simply due to the fact that he or she matriculated. Since the Ivy League graduate and the summa cum laude GPA are the rare exceptions, it is left to the rest of us to try and make the hiring decision a no-brainer for the recruiter based on our actual accomplishments.

The Famous 80/20 Rule Modified

Referring back to the 80/20 rule, when it comes to employment, I have slightly modified this to the 80/20/2 hiring rule. To be considered the top of the top, you not only need to prove that you are among the 20 percenters, you need to show that you are in the top 10 percent of the 20 percenters, which essentially puts you in the top 2 percent of the candidate pool. Look at the numbers. For each good job opportunity, a group of two hundred candidates usually send their resumes. Of the two hundred resumes sent, generally only five are brought in for a face-to-face interview. Five out of two hundred is 2.5 percent. Everybody else gets canned. On average, 97.5 percent of all candidates are eliminated at the resume screening.

It is our challenge to prove that we are the top-of-the-top job candidates, or we will be overlooked. That is where being part of the largest-ever deployment, best-ever success story, biggest-ever client capture, best product rollout, or first-ever attainment of a company goal is critical. Simple examples of being the best-of-the-best include being picked employee of the month/year/division. Perhaps you sold the most widgets in a month, or you handled the most phone calls in a week, or you met with twice as many students as an academic counselor, and so forth. I would say that over 60 percent of my clients have attained or have been part of one of these exceptional performance opportunities, so you have a good chance of having accomplished something significant like they did.

────────────────── **EXAMPLE 1** ──────────────────

His Resume Stated . . .

1991–1999 Global Securities
Senior Vice President of NASDAQ/OTC Trading
Responsible for making an orderly market in Global's top research covered stocks, initial stock offerings, institutionally covered stocks, and the most widely held Global stocks. Helped supervise other traders to ensure they complied with Global's trading parameters and trained new recruits.

My Rewrite Stated . . .

1991–1999 Senior VP, GLOBAL SECURITIES, INC.
Helped supervise a group of 20 traders who delivered $12–$15MM annually. My mandate was to deliver profit, mitigate losses, and lead the following projects.

Challenge	Global's CEO wanted my team to grow institutional business from 10% to 40% of revenues (originally 90% of revenues came from retail brokers).
Actions	Became a Top-3 Market Maker in 6 different stocks and built relations with Putnam, Wellington, Fidelity, and senior traders at Solomon, Merrill Lynch, and Prudential Securities.
Result	The relations I established with Wall Street banks helped launch Global's *first-ever* lead roles on 5 IPOs and co-lead on 40 other IPOs. Ultimately we doubled institutional business revenues from $2–$4MM.

> *The Key*—My client never tried to define a unique contribution in his eight-year work history as a Senior Vice President.
>
> *Change*—Global wanted to build its institutional banking business, and my client played a vital role in helping land the first-ever IPOs in Global's history.

———————————————— **EXAMPLE 2** ————————————————

His Resume Stated . . .

2000–Now   Verizon: Product Director
Responsible for the success of a cellular GSM product including its definition, development, launch, and P&L. Define product positioning, collect and organize requirements from the carriers and regions, validate requirements via global consumer research, coordinate the engineering teams of California, Singapore, India, and Florida, work with the field engineering teams to ensure carrier's ship acceptance, interpret financial reports, and coordinate pricing. Accomplishments: product development and launched in record time (before schedule), total revenues of $106 million and projected margin of $46 million in 6 months. First successful implementation of EMS, WAP 1.2 (Open Wave), SMS chat, Internal antenna, and so forth. Definition of MMS (Mobile Multi-media) and K-Java (J2ME) handsets.

My Rewrite Stated . . .

1994–present	**Verizon,** *Global Product Director* (Personal Communications Sector)
Goal	Launch an entry-level product that would be attractive to the budget-conscious consumer in Europe and America. The critical issue was that Verizon needed to be successful in the Low Tier market, which represents over 50% of all global cellular purchases.
Actions	• Coordinated global consumer research • Coordinated engineering teams and manufacturing facilities • Developed partnerships with added value parties—Open Wave, AOL
Result	Launched product in **record time** for Verizon (25% under projection)
Result	$106MM in revenues, 46% margin (Verizon's **best-ever** Low Tier launch)
Result	Drove engineer teams (2-U.S., 1-Singapore, 1-India) to reduce part count 15%
Result	Reduced production cost 30% by relocating from Singapore & Europe to China

---

The Key—This product director buried his stunning best-ever results beneath mundane tech-jargon.

Change—I carved out his four major results in a way that they are easily discernible by everyone who reads his resume.

RESUME QUALITY RATER RULE 5

Prove You Reduced Cost or Made Money for the Company

It is time to get very practical about your past contributions. Every business exists only on its ability to make a profit or reduce costs, by earning more than it spends or spending less than it earns. Even not-for-profits have to earn more than they spend to continue existing. A company's biggest fear is hiring employees who don't carry their own weight or justify their salary. Every time a corporate reorganization, rationalization, or downsizing occurs, the company is essentially trying to eliminate the staff who don't prove they are contributing. This may not seem fair, but it is a reality. When a hiring manager is looking for a new employee, he or she is looking for someone who can contribute in one of the two most obvious ways possible—either by helping the company make more money or work more efficiently, which saves money.

Since a hiring decision is an economic decision, it is worth breaking down the decision into component parts. First is your salary. Second are your benefits. Third is the budget of the department you would be responsible for managing, and last is the expectation or goals you are expected to achieve.

Calculating the Cost of a Hiring Decision

Example: To hire a manager of a convenience store. Pay = $50,000 per year with a benefits package equal to 25 percent of the salary (or $12,500). In addition, the new hire will manage a budget of $150,000, used to hire support staff and pay vendors and utility bills. The property is expected to gross $1,000,000 in sales. If you add up all the segments, this new hire is a $1,212,500 risk to the company.

That is a big bet being waged, and the bet needs to be justified in order to bring you into the company. To prove that the bet is safe, you need to show that you will deliver much more in value than the costs to hire you. That leads to the Meier 10-to-1 Rule.

The Meier 10-to-1 Rule

The rule simply states that your contribution should be worth ten times the cost of your salary and benefits. Let's say you earn $100,000 per year for your salary and $25,000 for the benefits. You need to try to prove to a potential company that your accomplishments saved or earned a total of $1,250,000. If you solve the 10-to-1 rule, you make their hiring decision a no-brainer. Who wouldn't want to hire somebody who added $1,250,000 in value at a mere cost of $125,000 per year?

One caveat I make to the Meier 10-to-1 Rule comes into play for clients who don't directly impact revenues or operating costs. In this situation, you need to look at the raw numbers of things you do impact. For example, if you were a librarian you might calculate the number of children who participated in your reading group. A teacher might look at the increase in grade average. A job counselor might note he excelled in finding work placements for the unemployed. You can always find ways to prove that you performed at a much higher productivity level than your peers.

Apple-to-Apple Comparison

One of the tricks I use is what I call an apple-to-apple comparison. If I were buying apples, which one would I want to pick? The juiciest, the freshest, and the biggest apples in the bunch, right? So, if there was a way to say that a particular apple was five days newer, was 10 percent bigger, and contained 15 percent more juice than the other ones, it would be a no-brainer to pick this apple. Likewise, we need to compare ourselves to our peers and find creative ways to carve out characteristics or results that demonstrate we are the best selection, the exceptional performer, and the best apple in the bunch.

─────────────────────── **EXAMPLE 1** ───────────────────────

His Resume Stated . . .

Bernard A. Mitchell Hospital, The University of Chicago Hospitals
Assistant to the Vice President, Clinical Services
Provided specialized financial and operational solutions to the Vice President of Inpatient services and the hospital's senior leadership staff.
- Selected accomplishments include: managed finances of clinical services including a $55 million operating budget and $1.7 million capital budget.
- Oversaw the complete implementation of the pharmacy management contract, yielding a $300,000 savings annually. Also, obtained the necessary pharmacy licensure.

My Rewrite Stated . . .

2000–2001 Assistant to the VP of Clinical Services
BERNARD A. MITCHELL HOSPITAL—DIVISION OF UNIVERSITY OF CHICAGO

Recruited to Cut Costs	Turned a revenue losing division into a profit center by providing financial and operational solutions to hospital senior leadership.
Action	Analyzed revenues, expenses, and cost variances at 53 cost centers representing 50% of Mitchell's $55M budget.
Action	Renegotiated provider service agreements that saved $1,050,000 per year.
Action	Minimized nurse agency usage across 32 departments by 68%.
Results	Reduced costs by $1.75 million within 6 months, which helped the University of Chicago sell Mitchell to Vanguard Health Systems in 2002.

The Key—His selected accomplishments neglected to show the *actions* he took to generate cost-saving results.

Change—I defined some actions to justify his results and then tied an important fact into the results, namely, the sale of the hospital to a competitor.

EXAMPLE 2

His Resume Stated . . .

Personal Experience

Northwestern Memorial Hospital   **Chicago, IL**   **May 1998–Current**

Business Manager   **Department of Rehabilitation—Occupational Therapy**

Marketing Coordinator   **Department of Otolaryngology—**
                      Head & Neck & Cosmetic Surgery

Corporate gift giving	Physician and patient advocate
Patient referral specialist	Clinical office manager
Referral tracking and database management	Physician Assistant

Patient Coordinator   **Department of Pediatric–Hematology/Oncology**

Reconstructed office policies and procedures	Determined section fee for services
Constructed, maintained, and oversaw billing	Audited daily clinical bills
Maximized reimbursement for insurance	Negotiated payment arrangements
Managed medical records	Credentialed physicians
Counseled patients with financial concerns	Solicited research funds

My Resume Stated . . .

5/98–Current   *Business Manager*   **NORTHWESTERN MEMORIAL HOSPITAL**

Recruited as the *first-ever* Business Manager for the *Rehabilitation Dept.* Manage a $10 million administrative budget and 75 staff. *The focus*—cut costs, build revenues, reorganize operations, raise staff productivity, and optimize reimbursements.

Challenge 1   Low utilization and productivity rates combined with periodic patterns of over- and understaffing.

- Response   Converted all salaried, nonmanagement staff to hourly and eliminated overtime.
- Benefit   Increased the utilization rate from 50% to 75%+; saved at least $50,000 in overtime pay.

The Key—My client's most impressive accomplishments were left completely unexplained.

Change—The overview builds appreciation for the challenges he met. I then wrote eight more response/benefits to define his value (I list only one).

RESUME QUALITY RATER RULE 6

Define Projects You've Led or Supported and Explain Results

The nature of a company is to think of itself organically, like a plant. Just as a plant bends toward the east side of the house to catch sunlight, a company constantly changes or adapts to economic realities and competitive pressures. It grows or contracts depending on internal changes such as the launch of an IPO or hiring a new CEO. External situations can be local in nature, like a change in construction zoning that may allow a potential customer to build in your region or the closing of a major account that causes your company to scramble for alternatives. Sometimes national changes in economic conditions push legislative reforms, advances in technology offer a competitive advantage, or foreign imports force a company to put together a team of its best and brightest employees to address a threat. Whatever the cause for change, a company is an entity that will constantly combine resources to meet the needs of the moment.

There is always some project or strategic rollout that corporations assign their staff to address. These dynamics mark a point when something important came about. Examples include implementing a new computer system, a new standard operating procedure for meeting a client's quality expectations, opening a new office, creating just-in-time processes to reduce on-hand inventory, launching a new product, or exporting products internationally.

The fact is that most professionals have contributed to projects in addition to their standard day-to-day work duties. You need to define your participation on the project, the goal of the project, and the results. Not only should we define personal results, but also the results the project delivered, preferably in money or efficiencies gained, to the company. I would say it is fair to assume that 80 percent of my resumes include projects, and as much as 50 percent of the content is project-centered.

A Live Example

One of my clients, a human resources trainer at Motorola before the tech-sector meltdown forced him to leave, had so many projects on his resume that he actually requested I take off the seventh and eighth projects, which I politely refused to do until he put it on the market. When he returned a year later, he told me he received two job offers because the companies liked what they read in his seventh project. The moral of the story is that the value of project participation can't be overemphasized.

The Secret of Projects

The key in using projects is to build toward a big conclusion. You need a bit of the old storyteller in you to tell enough about the focus or challenge that confronted you or the team to impress the reader that the rollout took special skill and dedication or had an important impact on the company. Also, remember that in every story there is a beginning, a middle, and an end. Most people don't include enough on some part of these three basic story elements to make their projects clear.

EXAMPLE 2

His Resume Stated . . .

1996–1997 Sales and Marketing Manager   FAR ACCESS Inc.
At FAR Access Inc. I led sales teams who developed Document Imaging Prospects as well as End-User and Large End-User of computer mass storage subsystems, including: Raids, MO Disk Storage, DLT & 3490E Tape Libraries, and Video Capture OEM systems. This company was the company that I had sold to an investment-oriented entrepreneur who was severely underfinanced. He had been offered business opportunities for document imaging that, when we tried to develop them, failed to materialize.

My Rewrite Stated . . .

1981–present   **VP Sales and Marketing   FAR ACCESS**
Negotiate exclusive territory agreements with corporate sales managers for a 3-state region of Illinois, Indiana, and Wisconsin. Target end users and manufacturers to create direct and pull-through sales impacting an aggregate of **$80MM** in revenues.

Project	**INTEL CORPORATION**—Won an exclusive contract for the IL, IN, WI region as a manufacturing rep for one of their lines. Managed 3 industrial distributors for the entire systems line encompassing 60 main products.
Keys	Sold technology concepts and cost-to-performance features, and trained the client on how to develop their own applications with Intel products.
Results	Growth doubled 4 years straight, from $0 to **$6.5MM** per year.

The Key—A fifty-five-year-old business owner closed his operation and wanted to find work with a large public corporation.

Change—The $80MM number is an end of the day quantity (what all his sales add up to). His exclusive contract with Intel is a home run.

EXAMPLE 2

His Resume Stated . . .

Napa Ridge Winery (Napa Valley, CA)
Wine Specialist
- Established relationships with VIP clientele and continued communication with renowned wine collectors.
- Appraised wines from regions around the world and created aggressive proposals for international clients.

My Rewrite Stated . . .

5/99–2001	**WINE SPECIALIST**	**Sotheby's**	Napa Valley, CA

Overview The first employee hired after Sotheby's acquired the auction house Davis & Co. to form America's largest wine auctioneer. — *My Role* — Establish relations with high-net-worth clients and wine collectors, appraise holdings, and craft proposals to make Sotheby's their auctioneer.

Project World's largest and most successful wine auction.

Actions Created catalog and tracking tools for the 4,000 lots auctioned. Arranged for customs clearance and shipment from UK to NYC. Supported all selling and marketing efforts with potential buyers.

Challenge Personally contacted 500+ international buyers and influential collectors to promote the auction and create intense interest.

Result *The Millennium Wine Sale* netted $14.4MM ($3MM over highest estimations).

The Key—He ignored his contribution to the world's largest wine auction.

Change—I focused on one of the most interesting projects I had ever learned about. I noted the value of the sale and the amount over projections that was attained.

RESUME QUALITY RATER RULE 7

Define How You Met Corporate Goals

This question focuses on accomplishing a goal that impacted the entire corporation, whether you were a team member or team leader. The key is that most corporate goals are tied to bottom line financial expectations. So, when you think of enterprise objectives, think of the financial impact to the company. The seventh rule is used to reveal the corporate staffer who contributes in some critical way to the success of the entire company. It is not as hard as you might think to elevate your profile to the corporate level, but you have to speak about the mission objectives of the company, the vision of the organization, and the goals that you and the team were pursuing.

Typical areas to focus on are dynamic transitions that confronted the company. A dynamic transition can be a merger and acquisition, a product launch, a line extension, a new business process, a migration of the IT system, or an implementation of a new business paradigm, and so forth. Think of dynamic shifts by considering anything that the company did to transition into a new way of doing business.

Two Live Examples

Since it is easier to explain this point via examples, I include the following two illustrations. The first one concerns how a retail manager impacted a $600 million company.

Example 1—When Hanes International opened their first-ever specialty store, my client was hired as the manager of the prototype store. He was expected to execute actions to ensure this first store would become the successful model for the eventual thirty-six-store nationwide rollout. What was compelling, as noted in the resume, is that Hanes expected to completely change their existing business model. Historically, Hanes sells their underwear product to other retailers, that is, Nordstrom, Marshall Fields, and so forth, or through Hanes discount outlets. In each case, profits are depressed because they don't capture the full MSRP (manufacturer's suggested retail price). With the new rollout of their own stand-alone specialty store, Hanes would charge full MSRP and add $75 to $100 million in new profit to the bottom line of the corporation. Interesting to think that a retail store manager could be part of building a $100 million profit stream.

Example 2—My client was a human resource manager for an industrial valve company, which had won a joint-partnership with Mobil Oil just prior to hiring him. Since his company had just achieved EDI capability (electronic data interface), it was able to, for the first time in company history, work directly with Mobil Oil. With this new account in hand, they needed to add 300 percent more staff and expand into four new states (FYI—the Fortune 500 often demand EDI capability from their business partners). His immediate role, as human resource manager, was to hire three times as much staff as the company had ever had on hand and do it intelligently so that they would not suffer from a poorly executed rapid expansion.

In both cases the idea was to elevate my clients' profiles by noting what was happening with the corporations that had hired them. If you elevate your contribution to the level of the entire enterprise, you build a much greater appreciation for your abilities by the potential hiring manager or executive recruiter.

Put the Puzzle Together

Think of your contribution similar to how a puzzle works. Although you might be part of a large corporation with a thousand employees, similar to a thousand-piece jigsaw puzzle, you only capture the reader's interest and motivate him or her to call if you paint your job piece, relative to the corporation's missions, goals, and objectives, compellingly. Another way to think of the puzzle analogy is to ask the question would you buy a jigsaw puzzle if the picture on the box cover only showed one piece of the puzzle and not the whole picture? Of course you wouldn't. The better the picture looks, the more desire it creates to put the puzzle together. Likewise, your resume has to have a snapshot of the entire enterprise along with a close-up of your specific contribution to help the hiring manager see how you could fit into his or her corporate puzzle.

EXAMPLE 1

His Resume Stated . . .

2/98–present	Senior Vice President—**Internal Audit, KELLER FINANCIAL**

My Rewrite Stated . . .

2/98–present	**Senior Vice President**—Internal Audit, KELLER FINANCIAL Analyze financial condition and prepare financial projections of an account portfolio with commitments totaling $250MM.
Project	**CORPORATE ACQUISITION**—coordinated due diligence efforts for the largest prospective acquisition in Keller's 80+ year-old history.
Focus	Created a tiered portfolio assessment strategy and led a team of 90 credit professionals to assess credit quality of a $14 billion commercial financial services company in one business week.
Result	Discoveries presented to executive committee led to the decision to decline the acquisition and protected Keller from bad debt risk.

The Key—My client literally listed his title (which he felt was enough to get him his next job).

Change—I highlighted his involvement in the most important potential acquisition in this multibillion-dollar corporation's history.

EXAMPLE 2

His Resume Stated . . .

March 96–Present
Special Projects Advisor, Petroleos De Venezuela (PDVSA) Caracas, Venezuela
Reporting to the manager of Specialized Processing Services, to Exploration Area Project Leaders, and to Oil Field Special Project Managers, I have been responsible for pre- and poststack depth-imaging projects over structurally complex areas. These

projects require cross-collaboration of processing and depth-imaging geophysicists, interpreters, geologists, and third-party contractors. I was the key player in the creation and development of technical standards for benchmarks, under which contractors would compete for PDVSA seismic processing contracts. I continue to participate in the many ensuing technical evaluation committees. I was a key contributor to the creation of PDVSA Geophysical Processing Computing Center.

My Rewrite Stated . . .

Project Manager—Venezuela Petroleum

Overview. . . Supervise technology projects for the Research & Technology Center that creates depth images of seismic data using high performance computers to find oil.

PROJECT 1	**LAKE MARACAIBO EXPLORATION**
Importance	Maracaibo is the largest oil region in Venezuela (1,000,000 barrels per day, or 33% of all production), worth $7.3 billion in yearly revenues.
Actions	Aggregated 10 years of seismic data gathered by 6 contractors to create a 3-D image used to find new well sites and optimize recovery.
Result (1)	Project completed 7 months ahead of schedule (this is probably the largest data-processing project of its kind in Latin America).
Result (2)	Delivered a 60 Gig, 3-D image that revealed a better correlation of recoverable oil and located potential wells.
Result (3)	PDVSA now captures 20% more oil with the same exploration budget.

The Key—My client, with a Ph.D. in seismology, oversold the technical nature of his work and ignored the bottom-line impact.

Change—I asked, "How does your work help the company?" The answer was startling. His seismic analysis increased the ROI on oil exploration by 20 percent.

RESUME QUALITY RATER RULE 8

Define How Each Job Progressed in Challenge and Responsibility

The important point here is to prove that your career is progressing and you are going from peak to peak, as opposed to having already peaked and are now on the decline. It is critical to prove that all of your past accomplishments were foundational steps to bring you closer to your full potential. You must, if at all possible, show that each job is a progression in responsibility and challenge.

The danger associated with allowing your career to look flat or on the decline cannot be overemphasized. I have supported hundreds of clients in the prime of their lives who dropped their salary by 25 percent to 75 percent simply because it looked like the proverbial tank of their career was on empty.

Often people are unaware when their career is stagnating or careening down the slippery slope of decline. Since they don't seem to notice the danger signs in general, it is only natural that they don't understand that prolonged career "plateauing," or decline, can irreparably damage future job prospects. Professionals find themselves in the danger zone for a variety of reasons. Some people have swung for the fences in the hope of hitting a home run on a risky venture (the dot-com era offered many such opportunities). Others attempted the entrepreneur route only to find that only one in ten start-ups ever achieve profitability. Others find their industry being consolidated, eliminated by the competition, the Internet, or technological advances. What's the point of telling you this? Because it's important for you to know the realities of how company recruiters categorize us, what indicates a downward spiraling career, and what can be done to overcome the problem.

Three Stages of a Career: Progress/Plateau/Decline

To begin to see where your career currently is, let's assume that a career can be broadly categorized into three key groups: progress, plateau, or decline. At the risk of oversimplification, a professional's career is assumed to be progressing if his or her job indicators include advancing titles, increasing salary, and increased staff or capital-budget management responsibilities. The next stage is the career plateau. Someone who is on a career plateau may have the following indicators: eight or more years with the same job title, stagnant salary growth, or lateral job changes (lack of advancement). The final stage, and the one that needs to be avoided at all costs, is the career that is in decline. Declining careers are typically represented by regressive job titles, lower salary, and obsolete industry expertise.

The best way to teach you how to position your career to indicate progress is to show an example of someone whose career is stuck in neutral or reverse.

A Live Example

Let me introduce you to Suzy Q. When I first met Suzy, I learned that with only a BA in political science she'd risen to the title of marketing manager for Ernst & Young within three years of graduating from school. Two years later, she was unceremoniously fired. From that point, she had become a temporary marketing staffer with Paladin Personnel. Her title was outsource marketing (which I later changed to marketing consultant). With Suzy, we have a thirty-three-year-old professional whose career is on the decline. Worse yet, she saw her new role as beneath her and subconsciously projected this in both her resume and in person. As an example, the first line of her resume read: "Coordinate logistics of National Restaurant Show booth for Alliance Food Service and Illinois Technology Showcase booth for Andersen Consulting (Ac)." To fix her problems I began to learn the projects she worked on for her Paladin clients.

As an aside, I always work from the perspective that the client adds value and adds it immediately. With this in mind, it is left for me to discover her value and prove that she was a key contributor, even if she is not a full-time employee. After studying her background, the first thing I discovered was the importance of what Ac was attempting to accomplish in February 2000. Suzy was originally sent to help two senior partners with their marketing efforts in a new department, Chicago's Dot-Com Launch Centre. Now, before you roll your eyes about the dot-com business world, don't forget that in June of 2000, according to the University of Texas at Austin's Center for Research in Electronic Commerce, Internet revenues soared to $523.9 billion. For Ac, it was critical to capture fee revenues from this burgeoning business. In fact, Suzy told me that Ac expected to generate 10 percent of their revenues from dot-com start-ups or dot-corp spin-offs (i.e., business segments carved from the Fortune 500). This would represent $1.3 billion in revenues within three years. Her role in building a billion-dollar-plus business unit was to assist the two partners in attaining the visibility required to be identified as dot-com experts. This included securing speaking engagements, sponsorships, and city and board appointments. To make this long story shorter, after I rewrote her resume, she was hired by KPMG as the associate marketing manager. The key was to tie her profile to the goals she was expected to help meet. This elevated her from a temp to a contributing professional deserving of promotion to an associate director of one of the largest consulting firms in the United States.

You can turn a sliding career into a progressive one by applying the old adage. Accentuate the positive and minimize the negative.

EXAMPLE 1

His Resume Stated . . .

June 1998–Present Web Research Assistant, American Medical Association: Chicago, IL
Responsible for responding to emails from consumers, tracking the review process for material on our website, and writing articles for the general public on various health topics. Also write reviews of other websites for our members.

April 1997–Present Editorial Assistant, American Medical Association: Chicago, IL
Assist in the production of consumer health books. Duties include proofreading, Internet and library research, manuscript tracking, correspondence with medical editors, and maintaining financial records of the department.

My Rewrite Stated . . .

EXPERIENCE

1997–Present	**American Medical Association**	Web Researcher	6/98–present
		Editorial Assistant	4/97–present

Originally assigned by the project editor to help produce 6 AMA books. Eventually the editor-in-chief contracted me to help build their web presence, which led me to double the AMA's web content.

Launched: *Health Insight*	• Site with 300+ pages averaging 150,000 page views/week
KidsHealth	• Site with 100+ pages averaging 7,000 page views/week
Write	Weekly KidsHealth Club Newsletter sent to 1,500 families
Write	Responses to health emails (average 20/day–1,500 to date)
Articles	• "Seeking a Second Medical Opinion"
	• "Men's Sexual Dysfunction"
Helped Produce	• Six consumer health books

───────────────────────── **EXAMPLE 2** ─────────────────────────

His Resume Stated . . .

Experience	Med Reports Plus, NY, NY
1999–2000	**Human Resources Assistant**
	Maintained personnel records, attendance and vacation schedules
	Interviewed and screened candidates
	Researched, selected, administered benefit enrollment
	Conducted systems and orientation training classes
1992–1999	**Training/Client Services Specialist**
	Responded to client inquiries via phone and email
	Trained clients on use of company software
	Processed client claims for third-party reimbursement

My Rewrite Stated . . .

1992–2000	**MED-REPORTS PLUS**	*HR Generalist*	1998–2000
		HR Trainer	1991–1998

Overview   As the first human resources generalist hired, I created all personnel standards and operating procedures used to build a business model to grow Med Reports from supporting 3 doctors to our current base of 100+ doctors located in competitive New York City.

Project 1	**STAFF TRAINING**	Taught staff how to organize and maintain records.
	• *Need*	As Med Reports grew 50% a year (number of clients and staff size), we needed to run an extremely efficient office.
	• *Result*	My standards improved timeliness, data maintenance, and processing of patient files.
Project 2	**STAFF RELATIONS**	Maintained open-door policy and counseled all associates each week for 5–20 minutes.
	• *Need*	It is critical for a small company in a competitive city like New York to keep recruiting costs modest by retaining staff.
	• *Result*	We remained fully staffed at relatively low salaries.

> *The Key*—My client listed his duties without connecting them to the larger corporate picture.
>
> *Change*—Projects are notable when they are juxtaposed to the overview, which notes the quick growth of this start-up in a competitive market.

RESUME QUALITY RATER RULE 9

Correlate What You've Done To Fit Your Career Objective

You must prove to the hiring manager that you are a great fit for the job he or she is trying to fill. This is where you need to tailor the body of the resume to fit the characteristics of the job. Tell the audience what they want to hear. In other words, make your career look like you are the obvious choice. For example if you are a dental hygienist who wants to become a medical sales representative, include all the service fees that you charge for your work and then add it up over a year's time and sum it into one big number (I call this an end of the day basket sweep). Another great way to fit your resume to the opening is to use the job advertisement and write your resume to hit the hiring managers' key points.

One of the easiest ways to get the career you want is to make your career objective job appropriate. Because people fear that a specific objective will pigeonhole them, many miss the boat on this point and fail to write a career objective that states anything specific.

Avoid Vague Objectives

Examples of objectives written by other resume-writing professionals:

1. *Focused and sales-oriented professional with expertise in motivating staff and clients. Knows medical terminology, etc.* (this client wanted to bridge from selling lingerie to pharmaceutical sales). I promise I did not make this up. This professional resume writer actually finished my client's objective with *etc*. **My rewrite:** *To continue a successful sales career by capitalizing on the ability to build a strong client base, increase profitability, and meet performance goals.*

Here is another favorite, also written by a professional resume writer.

2. *To have a position in a field where the management, personnel supervision, public relations, budget planning, and adherence skills that I possess are applicable.* This client wanted to continue a management career at a hotel. **My rewrite:** Hospitality management role where I will be challenged to streamline operations, increase profits, and reduce costs.

The key with the objective is to get to the point and state your strengths as appropriate to the field you are pursuing. Most resumes are written without an objective statement that sells them or a work history that proves they are good candidates for the position. Don't be afraid that you will pigeonhole yourself or lose out on opportunities if you are too specific in your objective. Consider the perspective of the hiring manager. On his or her desk at any given time are two hundred to five hundred resumes for each job opening. Their job is to cut this forest of resume stock down to a manageable finalist pool of ten to fifteen candidates who they will phone screen. Isn't it clear that, if they are looking for a salesperson, they need to read that you want to sell? You must tell the audience, in this case hiring managers, what they want to hear. This puts them at ease and supports their recommendation.

Along with a well-worded objective statement is the need to build a good correlative bridge to the job you want. This means you need to know what you want to do for a living. Now, here is where the rubber meets the road. People are so afraid of pinpointing what they want to do that they are very vague in their resumes.

Are You a Bridge or Ladder?

One of the best ways to become definitive in the resume is by identifying with one of the following two groups: the bridge professional or the ladder professional.

Bridge professionals want to change their employment field into an entirely new arena or an area that correlates to what they've done previously, but not exactly what they've done in the past. A dental hygienist who wants to go into pharmaceutical sales or a customer service rep who wants to become an account executive or a police officer who wants to go into contract negotiations are all bridge professionals. As I mentioned earlier, the key is to learn what the hiring manager wants to hear and then tell him or her you can do it. I counsel my clients to study job advertisements, highlight key phrases, read books on the topic to learn the jargon, and pick the mind of anyone they know who is in the field.

The *ladder professional* is a job seeker trying to progress to the next rung on the corporate ladder. An inside sales rep, known by the title of tele-sales rep or TSR, might want to become an account executive, the account executive might want to go to district sales management, a district sales manager might want to go to regional sales manager, and so forth.

For the ladder professional, the easiest way to use your resume to prove your job strengths correlate to your career objective is to communicate what your boss's boss knows. If you can speak at a level that is two steps above your current role and pinpoint what you've done to contribute to his or her goals, you will elevate your profile to attract that next hiring manager's attention. Once you are attractive to the boss's boss, you leapfrog the gatekeepers who want to keep you from taking their jobs. When you are trying to appeal to the boss's boss, you need to communicate the corporate strategies, regional strategies, and local strategies you supported, not just your immediate goals.

By crafting a targeted objective and correlating what you've done to meet the needs the employer is trying to fill, you make the employer's job easier and, in turn, increase your chance of being hired.

--- EXAMPLE 1 ---

His Resume Stated . . .

OFFERING

My quantitative skills as art director, graphic designer, and illustrator to create award-winning designs; excellent organizational skills; working with others as a team and my dedication and enthusiasm for designing and illustrating

1982–1988 1990–1999   The *Los Angeles Times*   LA, CA
Editorial Graphic Designer and Illustrator
- Responsible for designing feature covers, inside, and special sections, including: FASHION, DINING GUIDE, RELIGION, LYFESTYLE, GARDENING, and FOOD
- Directed photo set-ups for various feature covers
- Drawing editorial illustrations for all sections in newspaper

My Rewrite Stated . . .

1986–88/1990–99 Graphic Designer   The *Los Angeles Times* Newspaper

Overview   During 14 years of tenure with LA's most popular daily paper, I contributed on an editorial and artistic level by creating between 25% and 80% of all of the *Times*'s daily section cover pages. In addition, for over 6 years I directed photo set-ups for a total of 100 feature covers.

Challenge   Meeting daily deadlines for a team of 6 to 8 newspaper editors who had demanding expectations and personalities and were willing to sacrifice creative integrity and quality for expediency.

My Value   Produced 3 to 4 covers per day for a total of 10,000 section covers over 14 years. Additionally, I created 20 illustrations from scratch per month or 1,000 original drawings. Upon relocating to Chicago, a senior designer noted that I was replaced with 4 designers to handle my workload.

Contributions   Designed 10,000+ feature covers, inside and special sections for:

Fashion   over 4,000 cover pages designed
Dining Guide   new weekly section—40 cover pages designed
Religion   over 1,000 section cover pages designed
Lifestyle   over 2,500 section cover pages designed
Gardening   seasonal, over 1,000 section cover pages designed
Food   over 1,500 section cover pages designed

The Key—For ten years he was the sole editorial graphic designer for a top-twenty U.S. newspaper—yet you can't tell that in his description.

Change—I highlighted his important contributions and impressed the reader with amazing statistics.

—————————————— EXAMPLE 2 ——————————————

His Resume Stated . . .

Objective

To seek a management or sales position with a fast-growing company in the retail food industry so that I may utilize my 25+ years experience involving starting, operating, managing, and/or consulting in that industry.

Experience Highlights/Accomplishments

- Food preparations
- Have experience in sandwich preparation, short order cook, pizza making, and various full dinner entrees
- The nameless restaurant (1973–1983) dishwasher, promoted to assistant cook, promoted to head cook

Entrepreneur of Various Food Establishments

- Johnny's Deli/The Big Store (1985–1987) Berwyn, IL   Took over my family's grocery store and ran successful business until Aldi's moved into neighborhood.
- Positino's Pizza and Deli (1987–1990) Cicero, IL   Remodeled grocery store into a sit-down pizzeria and deli with delivery and pick-up service. Designed and laid out the floor plan, purchased all the equipment and supervised buildout. In addition, I designed the menu and the advertisement, did the hiring, accounting, and cooking. A fire terminated the business.

My Rewrite Stated . . .

Objective	Restaurant management where I can streamline operations, increase profits, and improve staff performance.
1987–1996 Owner/Operator, Positino's Inc.	• Positino's Pizzeria • Johnny's Deli • Vinnie Goomba's Italian Eatery
Overview	Positino's Inc. encompassed 3 unique restaurants ranging from a deli, pizzeria, family diner, to a full-service Italian restaurant.
Result	Grew revenues to $60,000 per month or **1,200%**
Recognition	*Sun Times*—Critic's Choice & *Food Industry News*—Silver Platter Award

---

The Key—A client who spent too much time explaining irrelevant facts that made him look bad.

Change—I focused on what it meant to open three restaurants in nine years by noting his industry recognition.

RESUME QUALITY RATER RULE 10

Demonstrate You Have a Good Professional Pedigree

This is the most straightforward point of all ten points (hence, I did not include examples). Since your career progression exists before you write your resume, this point simply notes that employers seek staff with a great work history, who went to good schools, and who maintain job continuity. Ironically, this area awards the least amount of points, namely, ten points versus fifteen points for the other questions. Even though some job seekers argue that their degree was all they needed to open doors of opportunity, or Fortune 500 experience gave them a leg up on the competition, if you accomplished nothing tangible in your career, you won't appeal to today's employer who needs to address bottom-line issues. The road is littered with burnouts who stagnated in their careers because they thought graduating from West Point in the 1950s meant something in the new millennium.

Why Is a Professional Pedigree Useful?

First of all, finding talented staff is usually conducted by a headhunter with very little time or an HR generalist who has to screen hundreds of resumes in order to pass the one-in-a-hundred keeper to other evaluators in the hiring chain. The initial screeners are not truly spending enough time to effectively evaluate your background to the fullest. Instead, they are looking for screening factors to make the initial cuts. Things like good Ivy League schools (employers are still impressed with tier-one academic credentials), good job title progression (otherwise known as fast-trackers), well-known Fortune 500 company names (aka "academy corporations"), and employment consistency (no significant gaps over the most recent ten-year work history) all indicate great professional pedigree.

If you are a new workforce entrant (meaning you haven't developed your professional pedigree), you have to note your internships, part-time jobs, summer work, assistantships, roles as a professor's assistant, and so forth. Even academic research is valid (meaning class work or student research projects that are relevant to your field). If you completed a bachelor's degree, but you went to three colleges to do it, don't write the other two colleges down, just the one where you completed your degree. If you did complete a four-year degree but also have a GED, you can eliminate the GED. I know this is obvious for most, and I think this is the one point that we can do the least to refine. Sometimes it's important to eliminate the junior college if it's a poorly recognized school.

Regarding a corporate pedigree, it is more important to note the more well-known corporate parent name than the division or business unit that paid your salary. For example, a director of human resources I recently helped worked for Material Sciences, a division of General Dynamics. He gave precedent to the subsidiary, Material Sciences, over General Dynamics the parent organization. I changed this to reflect the ordination according to name recognition as follows:

GENERAL DYNAMICS *Human Resource Manager—Material Sciences Division*

Another problem that can be fixed is when we find ourselves holding temporary jobs. For most of us, this feels like the professional kiss of death, but you can put the name of the company that you were assigned to and note that the assignment came through a job agency.

A similar issue is when you started with a temporary agency and then were hired full-time. Instead of giving yourself two job times, that is, Paladin Staffing assigned to Accenture from 10/02–5/03 and hired directly by Accenture in 5/03–present, the best thing would be to combine the two positions as follows: 10/02–present: Accenture (originally placed by Paladin Staffing until my contract was bought by Accenture in 5/03). This actually gives you a more steady work continuity and places the better-known corporate name in front of the recruiter.

PART 3

BEFORE AND AFTER RESUME EXAMPLES

CHAPTER FOUR
Resumes

There is no subject so old that something new cannot be said about it.

— Fyodor Dostoyevski, 1876

THE RESUME RATER IN ACTION

EXAMPLE

Client: Jeff Conway (see pages 53–62)
Before RQI Score: 45 Points = Power Puff
After RQI Score: 135 Points = Power Pro

Jeff's Situation

Jeff is a classic professional in career decline who had a top-heavy functional title, CFO (chief financial officer). What you have is a thirty-six year old whose first eight years of professional history included working for a Big-Six accounting firm, completing his CPA, and assuming two different senior financial analyst roles, one with Johnson & Johnson and one with Coca Cola Bottling. Then, all of a sudden, he quit to open a Subway sandwich shop (go figure). Two years later, he was back in the workforce and over the next five years landed with a company that nobody's ever heard of, Dream Vacations International. Two years later he became CFO of the Chicago branch of Adecco Temporary Staffing, a company few people would say is the same caliber as Johnson & Johnson or Coca Cola Bottling. For the sake of brevity, we will review only Jeff's most recent role as CFO of Adecco.

Factors Making Jeff's Score Low

His original RQI score of forty-five points is explained as follows. First, he never quantified any of his accomplishments for the Adecco job. I'm not sure what his first bullet point means, "Engineered turnaround of Accounting including creating policies and procedures, cleaning up account reconciliations, and revamping the financial reporting process." In relation to how his resume graded out, I was generous to give him any RQI points on questions one and four. On number three, he scored a zero, since he offered no evidence and only made claims. For number five he failed to define the tactics and strategies he used to accomplish his results. Actually he failed to have results in the first place. I was trying to be fair-minded to award him points on questions six and seven. Regarding question eight, I gave him the benefit of the doubt due to his high-ranking job title. When you look at question nine, it could be argued that he deserved either a yes or a some. I chose some because he did not prove that he warranted the role of a CFO at a Fortune 500 company, which was his goal. Finally, for number ten, I gave a yes, even though it could be argued that the smaller size of the companies defines him as a "declining," not "progressing," professional.

After the Rewrite (pages 59–61)

His after score of 135 points is a perfect RQI (note, any score over 120 actually should decrease your job search length). I uncovered six corporate critical challenges that he met in the two years since he was hired. In addition, I pinpointed $1,200,000 in savings he delivered to the company. It was interesting to see the sheer breadth of what he was involved with as a professional: everything from an acquisition, to a technology conversion, to new management compensation planning. Most of this was only alluded to or completely neglected in his original resume. If you do a before-and-after comparison, you will see nary a mention of the tax credit strategy he introduced that saved his company $400,000. You also won't see his reengineering of a management compensation plan that, before his restructuring, had caused senior managers to pursue non-core-competency business areas, which led to a reduction in income by 10 percent of Adecco's gross revenues.

To help you do a comparison, here is an accurate breakdown of his bullet points and our key challenges.

COMPARE

HIS RESUME		OUR REWRITE
His Seven Bullet Points	$\longleftrightarrow$	Our Six Challenges
Bullet One	=	Our Challenge One
Bullet Two	=	We Ignored
Bullet Three	=	Our Challenge Two
Bullet Four	=	Our Challenge Six
Bullet Five	=	We Ignored
Bullet Six	=	Our Challenge Three
Bullet Seven	=	We Ignored

Note: Our Challenges four and five he never addressed in the original.

So what happened? He received a $145,000 raise and became the VP finance and controller at Dun & Bradstreet. Hip, Hip, Hurrah!

HOW HOT IS YOUR RESUME?

Score its effectiveness

Resume Rater©

Name <u>Jeff Conway-Before</u>

2003, all rights reserved, Absolute Career Services

I. Does your resume. **PROVE YOUR VALUE**	Yes	No	Some
1. Define contributions <u>using numbers, percentages and statistics</u>	y ☒	N __	s __
2. Define <u>functional</u> tasks rather than <u>results</u>	y __	N __	s ☒
3. <u>Clearly</u> support your results with evidence	y __	N ☒	s __
4. Identify <u>largest, first-ever, top 20%</u> performance results	y __	N __	s ☒
5. <u>Prove</u> you helped reduce cost, earn money or add value to your company	y __	N __	s ☒

II. Does your resume. **PROVE YOU MET CORPORATE GOALS**			
6. Define projects you lead or supported and explain the results	y __	N __	s ☒
7. Explain corporate goals and how you helped meet those goals.	y __	N __	s ☒

III. Does your resume. **PROVE YOUR CAREER IS PROGRESSING**			
8. Define how each job progressed in challenge and responsibility	y __	N __	s ☒
9. Prove current job skills correlate to your career objective	y __	N __	s ☒
10. Show progressive titles, advanced education and good corporate pedigree.	y ☒	N __	s __

Each 10 points below a virtuous resume score of 120 points adds 1-to-2 weeks of search time to your job hunt (this is added on top of the standard length of 1 month per $10,000 in base salary you expect to earn).

Example: Your score = 60 (120 - 60 = 60)
          You scored 60 points below 120
Problem   You're adding 6 to 12 weeks to your job search

Score 60 /your resume has	
120-135	Power Pro
100-120	Power Prospect
85-100	Power Pansy
under 85	Power Puff

Jeff Conway
2730 N. Fairway
New York, NY 10002
212-821-2976

PROFILE

A CPA with over fourteen years of well-rounded finance and accounting experience encompassing several industries including manufacturing, hospitality, retail, temporary staffing, and public accounting. Has consistently demonstrated a "hands on" entrepreneurial spirit, a strong sense of internal controls and cost management, and an ability to manage and develop talent.

PROFESSIONAL EXPERIENCE

ADECCO. (1997 to present)—Adecco *of Chicago, the oldest and largest franchise of Adecco corporation, is a temporary staffing leader in the Chicagoland area with over $75 million in annual revenue and in excess of 35,000 employees per year. Adecco provides permanent and temporary staffing for the clerical, light industrial and professional business sectors.*

<u>**Chief Financial Officer/ Treasurer**</u> Manage 15 people performing functions including Accounting, Credit, Payroll, and Risk Management.

- Engineered turnaround of Accounting including creating policies and procedures, cleaning up account reconciliations, and revamping the financial reporting process.
- Developed full line item budget process and streamlined into overall strategic planning process.
- Performed financial review and supervised due diligence of business acquisitions.
- Represent company as board member for Captive insurance company. Created team management concept to manage risk resulting in a significant reduction in claims.
- Revamped cash management processes and strategy.
- Installed new server based payroll/billing system.
- Member of TEC

DREAM VACATIONS INTL. *(1995 to 1997)—Dream Vacations Intl., affiliated with SAM ZELL 'S EQUITY GROUP, is the largest American owned and operated passenger cruiseline including, THE DELTA QUEEN STEAMBOAT CO. and AMERICAN HAWAII CRUISES, and specializes in providing unique vacation experiences. The company is publicly traded on Nasdaq (AMCV) and has approximately $190 million in Revenue.*

<u>**Controller**</u>—Manage a staff of 10 people performing functions including Revenue, Accounts Payable, Payroll, General Accounting, Consolidations and Treasury.

- Worked with the CEO, President, and VP Finance on a daily basis concerning critical business issues.
- Worked with senior management to develop strategy and provide analysis for plan that significantly reduced SG&A expenses and improved overall company profitability. This process yielded millions in SG&A savings and a year-to-year improvement in operating income of $21 million.
- Implemented and managed cash investment function.
- Managed general ledger conversion on DBS (Dynamic Business Systems).
- Key financial contact for risk management functions. Critical member of cross-functional team assembled to prepare largest business interruption claim in company history. Claim resolution represented *35%* of company operating income.

SBD INCORPORATED (1993 to 1995) - *Established corporation to own and operate a Subwav Sandwich store. Set up S-Corp in state of New York, secured financing through the Small Business Administration, analyzed site area demographics and market potential, set up a marketing plan and overall business strategy, and developed staff and store management until operation became self-sufficient. Not currently involved with day-to-day operations.*

COCA COLA BOTTLING COMPANY (1990 to 1993)—*Coca Cola is a multi-billion dollar supplier of packaging products.*

Senior <u>**Financial Analyst**</u>—Responsible for the consolidation and analysis of results for the FLEXIBLE PACKAGING Division. Total division revenue was approximately $500 million. Interfaced daily with senior management, summarized and analyzed financial results for ten manufacturing facilities, prepared monthly forecast and margin analysis, prepared budgets and long-range plan, and responsible for all reserve analysis.

<u>CCB 2000 Team</u>—CCB 2000 was a cross functional team aligned with the consulting firm A. T. KEARNEY whose mission was to streamline SG&A expenses and strategically align CCB to be competitive into the 21st century. Performed all financial analysis to support the team and reported to the team leader.

<u>**Principal Auditor**</u>—Supervised operational audits including Purchasing, Capital Acquisitions, Research & Development, and Licensing Agreements.

JOHNSON & JOHNSON (1988 to 1990)—Johnson & Johnson is a multi-billion dollar supplier of hospital products and services.

Senior <u>**Financial Analyst**</u>—Responsible for the coordination and review of the operating plan for the CONVERTERS/CUSTOM STERILE manufacturing facilities in El Paso Texas. Consistent with other US companies in the Maquiladora industry Johnson & Johnson had one manufacturing facility in El Paso, Texas on the border and three facilities in Mexico where inexpensive labor was utilized. This was Johnson & Johnson's largest manufacturing facility in the United States. Organized, planned and reviewed operating plan for all four manufacturing facilities, performed IRR analysis for all capital acquisitions including lease/buy decisions, played a critical role with the formation of product costs and the review of manufacturing variances and established fixed asset procedures.

<u>**Financial Analyst**</u>—The Operating Room Division generated approximately $600 million in revenue manufacturing and distributing products for the operating room under the brand names of CONVERTERS/CUSTOM STERILE and V. MUELLER. Responsible for the review and analysis of financial results for division, prepared and analyzed transfer pricing procedures, assisted with the preparation of year-end reports including the tax package, and prepared account reconciliation's.

ERNST YOUNG & CO. (1985 to 1988)

<u>**Senior Auditor**</u>—Planned and supervised audits of two to four employees, prepared time budgets, plans and programs, client base included manufacturing, retail, financial services, and governmental, prepared original footnote disclosure.

EDUCATION
UNIVERSITY SOUTHERN CALIFORNIA, Los Angeles, CA—BS Accounting – 1985
CERTIFIED PUBLIC ACCOUNTANT—November, 1988

Resume Rater©

HOW HOT IS YOUR RESUME?

Score its effectiveness

Name _Jeff Conway-After_

I. Does your resume.... **PROVE YOUR VALUE**	Yes	No	Some
1. Define contributions <u>using numbers, percentages and statistics</u>	y ☒	N __	S __
2. Define <u>functional</u> tasks rather than <u>results</u>	y __	N ☒	S __
3. <u>Clearly</u> support your results with evidence	y ☒	N __	S __
4. Identify <u>largest, first-ever, top 20%</u> performance results	y ☒	N __	S __
5. <u>Prove</u> you helped reduce cost, earn money or add value to your company	y ☒	N __	S __

II. Does your resume.... **PROVE YOU MET CORPORATE GOALS**			
6. Define projects you led or supported and explain the results	y ☒	N __	S __
7. Explain corporate goals and how you helped meet those goals.	y ☒	N __	S __

III. Does your resume.... **PROVE YOUR CAREER IS PROGRESSING**			
8. Define how each job progressed in challenge and responsibility	y ☒	N __	S __
9. Prove current job skills correlate to your career objective	y ☒	N __	S __
10. Show progressive titles, advanced education and good corporate pedigree.	y ☒	N __	S __

Each 10 points below a virtuous resume score of 120 points adds 1-to-2 weeks of search time to your job hunt (this is added on top of the standard length of 1 month per $10,000 in base salary you expect to earn).

Example: Your score = _135_ (120 - _135_ = _-15_)

You scored _-15_ points below 120

Problem You're adding _-1.5_ to _-3_ weeks to your job search

Score _135_ /your resume has	
120-135	Power Pro
100-120	Power Prospect
85-100	Power Pansy
under 85	Power Puff

JEFF CONWAY

2730 N. Fairway, New York, NY 10002 ☎ 212-821-2976

OBJECTIVE   To continue a successful executive finance career for a company that is aggressively competing for market share, executing acquisition strategies, or restructuring business operations.

EXPERIENCE

1997–present   ***Chief Financial Officer/Treasurer***   **ADECCO**

Recruited by the CEO to overhaul accounting and financial systems and prepare the company for an aggressive corporate ***acquisition strategy*** projected to double the company in 5 years. Manage 15 staff who support 25 offices and 2 business units. Additionally, I act as in-house legal counsel, plan administrator of the 401(k), and board member for our captive insurance company.

Challenge ① **NEW ACCOUNTING SYSTEM INFRASTRUCTURE**: Inadequate accounting controls, operating procedures, and financial records caused internal chaos.

Solution   Hired all new accounting staff while reducing head count 20%, then implemented new accounting, reconciliation, cash management, financial reporting, and line item budget systems.

Challenge ② **MERGER & ACQUISITION**: Performed due diligence to assess value and determine whether company should complete a new business acquisition.

Solution   Analysis has led to a successful acquisition that exceeded profit projections.

Challenge ③ **TECHNOLOGY SYSTEMS CONVERSION**: As part of a 7-franchisee consortium, I directed our technology consulting firm as we converted from IBM AS400 to an NT Client Server environment.

Solution   Managed 66% of the project implementation and delivered final phase to SVP of Operations.

Challenge ④ **TAX CREDIT STRATEGIES**: Capitalized on new federal legislation offering welfare to work incentives.

Solution   Hired a tax credit consulting firm and worked with them to create programs that captured **$400K** in first six months and is projected to earn **$1MM** annually by 4Q2000.

Challenge ⑤ **MANAGEMENT COMPENSATION/INCENTIVE PLAN**: Existing bonuses motivated business development managers to pursue non-core business, which dropped key sector income by 10%.

Solution   Worked with CEO and VP of HR to create new compensation plans, which grew revenues in our core strengths.

Challenge ⑥ **RISK MANAGEMENT PROGRAM:** A 50% jump in worker's compensation claims prior to my hire caused unease with Milestone, Inc., our captive insurance company.

Solution   Created a risk management structure and a worker's compensation team, and selected a manager of planning analysis who reduced claims by **$800K** over two years.

1995–1997   *Controller*   **DREAM VACATIONS INTL.**
[Part of Sam Zell's Equity Group. The largest US passenger cruise-line, with two entities: the Delta Queen Steamboat Co. & American Hawaii Cruise]
Part of a new management team tasked with reducing SG&A expenses, improving profitability and operating income by **$21MM**. Managed 10 AP, payroll, accounting, treasury, and revenue staff.

Challenge ⑦   A total accounting cleanup of an operation lacking reliable reporting systems, accounting integrity, or the financial statement tools that are needed to run and grow the business.

Solution   Forensic accounting recovered **$1MM**: Saved in overpayments to vendors, **$150K** in double refunds to customers, **$800K** in prebought airline tickets, and reduced A/R from **$750K** to **$2.5K**.
Designed first corporate cash management program.

PROJECT ①   FINANCIAL PLANNING TO RAISE NEW CAPITAL
Dream Vacations needed to raise in excess of a billion dollars to finance new ships and leverage their Hawaiian cruise monopoly, a result of being the only US flagged cruise line in existence (protected by the Passenger Vessel Act of 1886). I analyzed costs in the existing cruise line, scheduled a 5-year revenue forecast, and recommended financial strategies.

Result   Provided the financial analysis to senior management that resulted in eliminating underperforming assets and saved **$21MM,** thereby making the company profitable for the first time in 10 years. My analysis helped secure **$40MM** of US-backed bonds guaranteed by the Maritime Administration.

PROJECT ②   PREPARED NEGOTIATIONS FOR THE LARGEST BUSINESS INTERRUPTION CLAIM IN COMPANY HISTORY
After high waters trapped our largest steamboat and canceled 6 cruises. My role: analyzing all possible business impact and preparing a unique *lost opportunity/lost revenue* negotiation stance.

Result   Claim award was **$1.8MM** (35% of company's FY 96 operating income—300% over CFO's projection).

PROJECT ③   CHANGE MANAGEMENT—CORPORATE H.Q. RELOCATION TO FLORIDA FROM NEW YORK
Helped consolidate Dream Vacations Intl.'s two regional offices into a central site. My role was maintaining business operations at a high level while staff morale declined rapidly.

Result   Seamless relocation while 70% of New York accounting staff was eliminated.

1993–1995   *Owner*   **SBD, INC.**
Purchased a Subway franchise. Set up S-Corp in New York. Secured financing through the Small Business Administration, analyzed demographics, and wrote marketing plan.

1990–1993   *Senior Financial Analyst*   **COCA COLA BOTTLING COMPANY**
A *$4.5BB supplier of bottling products.*
Analyzed and summarized monthly forecasts, margin analysis, and long-range reserve plans for this **$500MM** FLEXIBLE PACKAGING division, which included 10 manufacturing facilities.

PROJECT ④   CCB 2000 Team   POST MERGER ACTIVITY —
Pechiney purchased CCB from Triangle Holding Corp., hired A. T. KEARNEY, then assembled a team of executives to streamline all support functions while increasing productivity by creating a *shared services* environment for the 7 business segments and 15,000 employees.

Result   Selected by CCB 2000 Team President to prepare all financial analysis for four team cells: MIS/R&D, Marketing/Sales, Finance, and H.R. Once approved by the CEO and Board of Directors, project went forward to phase II.

Jeff Conway

1988–1990	***Senior Financial Analyst***	**JOHNSON & JOHNSON**

Johnson & Johnson is a $5BB international supplier of hospital products and services.
Hired as part of the new finance team after a merger between *Converters/Custom Sterile* and *V. Mueller* creating the **$600MM** *Operating Room Division*. Within two weeks of promotion to senior financial analyst, I made a group presentation to 40 department heads outlining business plans for the El Paso manufacturing plant (Johnson & Johnson's largest in the United States) and 3 other Mexican maquiladora locations.

PROJECT ⑤   STRATEGIC PLANNING OF CAPITAL INVESTMENTS AND CAPACITY EXPANSION WITHIN MEXICO AND THE UNITED STATES
Analyzed cost of capital, labor, and final product delivery to determine plant expansion in Mexico.
Result   Johnson & Johnson invested **$40MM** to expand in Mexico.

1985–1988	***Senior Auditor***	**ERNST & YOUNG (formerly Arthur Young),** Los Angeles, CA

EDUCATION   BS Accounting—University Southern California, Los Angeles, CA   **1986**
CERTIFICATION   C.P.A.   **1988**

JEFF CONWAY'S STORY

Success Snapshot: Eight weeks after I wrote his resume, Dun & Bradstreet hired him as VP finance and controller—$145K raise.

Career Sweet Spot: Turnaround of a failing career and launch into the executive ranks of a well-known media company without prior industry experience.

Trouble Spot Fixed: Jeff's career was declining. After jobs with Ernst & Young, Johnson & Johnson, and Adecco, Jeff opened a Subway. His next job was at Dream Vacations Intl., a no-name company that led to Adecco's temporary staffing.

To Use This Chart:
1. Score your resume.
2. Find Before and After RQI scores in the PYV, MCG, and CPS categories similar to your scores.
3. Strengthen your weaknesses using our tactics.

BEFORE SCORE			of 100%	Score
Category I	Prove Your Value	PYV = 0%		15 of 75
Category II	Met Corporate Goals	MCG = 16%		10 of 30
Category III	Career Progress Status	CPS = 33%		20 of 30
	Their RQI Score:		11%	**45 of 135**

AFTER SCORE			of 100%	Score
Category I	Prove Your Value	PYV = 87%		75 of 75
Category II	Met Corporate Goals	MCG = 100%		30 of 30
Category III	Career Progress Status	CPS = 100%		30 of 30
	Our RQI Score:		100%	**135 of 135**

CAREER STATS

Career Field:	Temporary Staffing
Old Title:	CFO
New Title:	VP, Controller
Bridge or Ladder:	Bridge to Media

IMPROVEMENT

From:	Power Puff
To:	Power Prospect

KEY

Power Pro:	95% RQI	Power Pansy:	60–80% RQI
Power Prospect:	80–95% RQI	Power Puff:	Below 60% RQI

AARON PARKER

Recent College Graduate

CAREER HIGHLIGHTS

- Salary increase with his new resume: $38,500

- Promoted from unemployed recent college graduate to coordinator of international business development

- Job search length: two weeks

BEFORE

RQI: 15

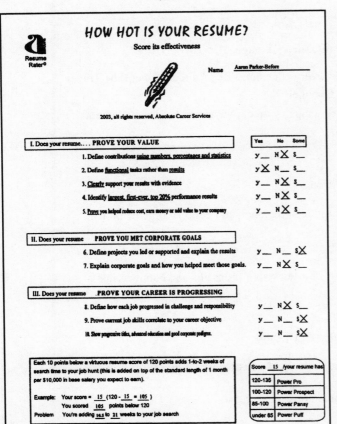

AFTER

RQI: 120

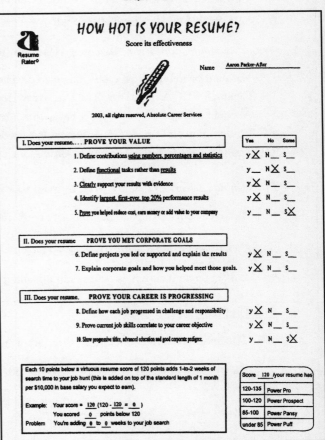

AARON PARKER
1233 Tomland Drive
Denver, CO 80439
303-279-1356
aparker@hotmail.com

STRENGTHS:

Bottom-line emphasis; manage and supervise people and projects; team player and team builder; maintain effective working relationships with managers, co-workers, clients and the public.

Marketing, sales, advertising, and promotional skills utilized in every position held.

Learn new areas quickly; writing and presentation skills; detail oriented and accurate; computer skills (Windows, Excel, Access, ACT, PowerPoint, Internet, and other areas).

EXPERIENCE:

Industrial Real Estate Sales Associate, **Triangle Realty, Denver, CO** *(5/01–1/02)*

- State and Nationally licensed real estate salesperson
- Market expert of industrial real estate in Northern Counties (including warehouses, manufacturing plants, and research and development facilities).
- New business development in Northern Counties.
- Cold calling and telephone marketing and promotion experience.

Senior Account Coordinator, **Discovery Communications, Inc., Chicago, IL** *(10/99–1/01)*

- National commercial accounts managed on The Discovery Channel, TLC, Animal Planet, The Travel Channel, BBC America and The Discovery Health Channel.
- Account management on a daily basis with advertising agency media buyers and individual clients.
- Competition analysis (of other top cable networks).
- Trained 4 newly hired Account Coordinators.

Promotional/Advertising, **Club Mix, Denver, CO** *(12/98–5/99)*

- Marketed sponsorships of campus nightclub events to local, regional, and national organizations.

Intern, **Denver Transfer/Edit, Denver, CO** *(6/97–8/97)*

- Post-production activities (sales, editing, and graphics for television programs and commercials).

EDUCATION

B.A., Telecommunications/Sociology, Colorado University, CO *(8/99)*

- *Chair* (Social and pledge activities, recycling), **Sigma Alpha Mu Fraternity** ('96 –'99)

— References available upon request —

Aaron P. Parker

1233 Tomland Drive Denver, CO 60439 303-279-1356 Parker@aol.com

SUMMARY

Maintain client relations, develop new business opportunities, and focus on presenting opportunities and communicating risk factors. Possess excellent networking, analytical, problem-solving, and communication skills. My key emphasis is to build client loyalty by executing my duties efficiently, diligently, and in a manner to achieve profits.

BUSINESS EXPERIENCE

5/01–1/02
Overview

Sales Associate   **Triangle Realty, Denver, CO**
Recruited by the director of sales in a business development role where I aggressively marketed Epic's industrial real estate portfolio or uncovered lease/purchase opportunities to help manufacturers find warehouse, production plants, and R&D facilities.

Challenge   As the junior team member on a staff of 25, it was my role to cold-call and set appointments. This led to an aggressive prospecting plan that netted an average of 10–12 meetings a week with company presidents, CFOs, and real estate brokers.

Results   Developed a base of 300 contacts that included uncovering 15 opportunities: 9 sellers and 6 buyers seeking sites between 10,000 and 70,000 square feet with contract values up to $2 million.

10/99–1/01
Overview

Senior Account Coordinator   **Discovery Communications Inc., New York, NY**
Part of a 3-person account team (executive, planner, and coordinator) that supported advertising agency media buyers and Fortune 500 clients by selling air time on the following channels:
• The Discovery Channel   • Animal Planet   • BBC America
• The Travel Channel   • TLC   • The Discovery Health Channel

Challenge   Coordinating an average of 6 international advertising agencies and 20 corporate clients (i.e., Dreamworks, TGI Friday's, Ralston Purina, Sears, and MasterCard) who bought thousands of cable spots on 6 unique channels.

Result   Handled client reporting, media scheduling, and make-good negotiations so well that my account executive could focus solely on selling, which allowed him to be the #1 AE in the Midwest (we were the only selling team never to be restructured).

Project   Trained all newly hired account coordinators during my tenure.

12/98–5/99
Overview

Promotional/Advertising   **Club Mix, Denver, CO**
Originated, pitched, and negotiated with the GM of Denver's largest nightclub, a promotional marketing program to increase business on their off nights.

Challenge   Securing sponsorships from a national magazine, national brewery and distiller, as well as local businesses to financially support key events.

Results   Grew door receipts 500% by the first event and another 40% by the third event.

EDUCATION   1999   B.A., Media Communications/Sociology COLORADO UNIVERSITY, Denver, CO
                  Chair   Social and pledge activities   SIGMA ALPHA MU

AARON PARKER'S STORY

Success Snapshot: Two weeks after I wrote Aaron's resume, McGraw Hill made him their coordinator of international business development. He liked breaking into publishing and international business.

Career Sweet Spot: Three years out of college, fired at two jobs, and lasting only seven months as a commercial realtor who never closed a deal. Then, after my resume rewrite, he was hired to coordinate a multimillion dollar international trade division of a book publishing company.

Trouble Spot Fixed: Overcame the stigma of being fired and lack of industry knowledge in publishing.

To Use This Chart:
1. Score your resume.
2. Find Before and After RQI scores in the PYV, MCG, and CPS categories similar to your scores.
3. Strengthen your weaknesses using our tactics.

BEFORE SCORE			of 100%	Score
Category I	Prove Your Value	PYV = 0%		0 of 75
Category II	Met Corporate Goals	MCG = 16%		5 of 30
Category III	Career Progress Status	CPS = 33%		10 of 30
	Their RQI Score:		**11%**	**15 of 135**

AFTER SCORE			of 100%	Score
Category I	Prove Your Value	PYV = 87%		65 of 75
Category II	Met Corporate Goals	MCG = 100%		30 of 30
Category III	Career Progress Status	CPS = 100%		25 of 30
	Our RQI Score:		**89%**	**120 of 135**

CAREER STATS

Career Field:	Sales
Old Title:	Real Estate Agent
New Title:	Coordinator Int'l Bus.
Bridge or Ladder:	Ladder and Bridge

IMPROVEMENT

From:	Power Puff
To:	Power Prospect

KEY

Power Pro:	95% RQI	Power Pansy:	60–80% RQI
Power Prospect:	80–95% RQI	Power Puff:	Below 60% RQI

SAM BENTLY

High-Tech Transfer

CAREER HIGHLIGHTS

- Salary increase with his new resume:
  $50,000 + bonus potential to $145,000

- Promoted to account executive, flowers.com

- Job search length: one week

BEFORE

RQI: 40

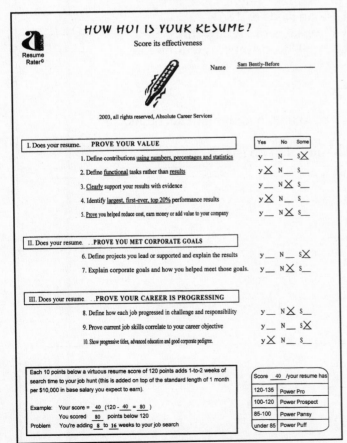

AFTER

RQI: 120

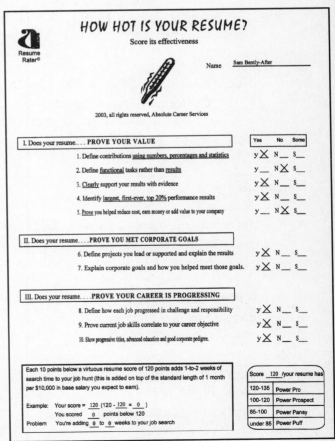

Sam Bently
2890 Forest View Drive
Glenview, IL 66061
847.247.8291

Professional Experience

US Robotics Inc., 2000–2001, Chicago, IL
Sales Representative
- Specialized in sales of software that controls cameras over the Internet
- Targeted customers in two vertical markets; Media and Enterprise
- Responsibilities included: prospecting clients, client specific sales presentations, closing sales, and managing accounts
- Worked with project engineers to improve product offering
- Adapted to continually changing technological environments

Motorola Inc., 1999–2000, Arlington Heights, IL
Global Satellite Solutions Group (Indium Satellite Group)
Account Manager
- Specialized in sales of Iridium satellite equipment and service
- Prospected new accounts ranging from individual sales to Fortune 500 companies
- Responsible for entire sales cycle: initial call, sales presentation, close of sales, product training, and problem solving
  - 1999   Finished 14th in sales of 186
  - Finished 4th in sales of all new hires
  - Maintained a 98% customer retention rate

Wells Fargo Bank, 1996–1998, Tucson, AZ
Customer Service Agent
- Responsible for opening new accounts, maintaining accounts, and customer service
- Accountable for over $35,000 on a daily basis

Education

University of Arizona, Tucson, AZ (1994–1998)
Bachelor of Business Administration
Majors: Finance and Spanish

Madrid, Spain (1996)
Intense Spanish Language Courses

Tools

Microsoft Office
Adobe Photoshop
Excellent Spanish language skills

SAM BENTLY

2890 Forest View Drive, Glenview, IL   66061   847-247-8291

OBJECTIVE   To continue a successful sales career.

EXPERIENCE
2002–2003   *Sales Representative*   **GE LONG-TERM CARE INSURANCE**   Chicago, IL
                *Overview......*Sell long-term care products to the senior market. Selling strategy was setting 1–2 seminars a week and cold-calling 150–200 individuals from a prospect list to build attendance.

Result   Sales Rookie of the Month: 11/02

2000–2001   *Sales Representative*   **U.S. ROBOTICS INC.**   Chicago, IL
                *Overview......*Targeted customers in 4 market categories: professional sports, media, institutional, and construction. Prospected for new clients, made sales presentations, closed sales, and managed accounts. Worked with project technical engineers to improve product offering.

                Challenge   Selling *TrueLook* software and web camera packages costing $10,000–$120,000 each.
                Tactic 1   Work with directors of sports marketing, promotional managers, and advertising managers to bundle our product with their existing marketing or advertising sponsorships and drive consumer viewership of professional sports.
                Tactic 2   Demonstrate how construction project managers could remotely track progress stages of large-scale building projects.
                Tactic 3   Work with multimedia conglomerates to promote national events and contests.

Results   Initiated or developed relationships with the following clients:

Sports	**MLB**	• Cubs	• White Sox	• Pirates	• SF Giants
	NBA	• Bulls	• Raptors	• Nuggets	• Mavericks
		• NBA Finals		• NBA All-Star Game	
	NHL	• Blackhawks	• Penguins	• Maple Leafs	• Avalanche
	Int'l Soccer	• Leeds United	• Everton	• Celtic	• Manchester
		• Coventry City	• Fulham	• Chelsea	• Glasgow Rangers
Schools		• Harvard Univ.	• Northwestern Univ.		
		• Univ. of CO	• Univ. of AZ	• Univ. of GA	• Univ. of IL
Building		• E-IDC • Hyatt Hotels	• Harza Engineering		
Media		• Clear Channel Communications (10 cameras to rotating locations)			

1999–2000   *Account Sales Manager*   **MOTOROLA INC.**   Arlington Heights, IL
                *Overview......*Recruited as part of an elite international sales force six months after the launch of the $11 billion Iridium Satellite communication network.

                Challenge   Selling equipment and services to a global market.
                Tactic 1   Uncovered clients willing to pay $3,500 for an Iridium phone or $1,000 for a pager to conduct their international business.
                Tactic 2   Managed full sales cycle: initial call, sales presentation, closing the sale, product training, and technical problem solving.

Results   Sold to: Sample of industries penetrated • Pharmaceutical Industry: Baxter and Abbott Labs
                                                        • Extreme Adventure: Charlie's Safaris
                                                        • Corporate: Service Master

Results   Finished the #4 top seller on a team of 50 sales representatives.

EDUCATION   1998   Bachelor of Business Administration Finance, University of Arizona, Tucson, AZ
                  Sports: University Arizona Soccer Team 1995–98
                  2001–02:   Intense Spanish Language Courses, Sevilla, Spain

SAM BENTLY'S STORY

Success Snapshot: Sam worked at a dot-com that failed. He then sold life insurance. Within a week of sending his resume to recruiters, he received three job offers. The job he accepted was selling software for flowers.com. He now earns a $50,000 base salary plus bonus. If he hits his sales plan his salary will grow to $145,000.

Career Sweet Spot: Quick job search. In addition, I helped him get out of 100% commissioned insurance sales.

Trouble Spot Fixed: Making a dot-com technology victim appeal to another corporation.

To Use This Chart:
1. Score your resume.
2. Find Before and After RQI scores in the PYV, MCG, and CPS categories similar to your scores.
3. Strengthen your weaknesses using our tactics.

BEFORE SCORE			of 100%	Score
Category I	Prove Your Value	PYV = 26%		20 of 75
Category II	Met Corporate Goals	MCG = 16%		5 of 30
Category III	Career Progress Status	CPS = 50%		15 of 30
Their RQI Score:			**30%**	**40 of 135**

AFTER SCORE			of 100%	Score
Category I	Prove Your Value	PYV = 80%		60 of 75
Category II	Met Corporate Goals	MCG = 100%		30 of 30
Category III	Career Progress Status	CPS = 100%		30 of 30
Our RQI Score:			**89%**	**120 of 135**

CAREER STATS

Career Field:	Sales
Old Title:	Insurance Sales Rep
New Title:	Account Exec. FTD
Bridge or Ladder:	Ladder

IMPROVEMENT

From:	Power Puff
To:	Power Prospect

KEY

Power Pro:	95% RQI	Power Pansy:	60–80% RQI
Power Prospect:	80–95% RQI	Power Puff:	Below 60% RQI

JIM LAMBERT

Franchisee to Corporate

CAREER HIGHLIGHTS

- Moved into an entirely new industry

- Promoted to financial consultant

- Job search length: ten weeks

BEFORE

RQI: 55

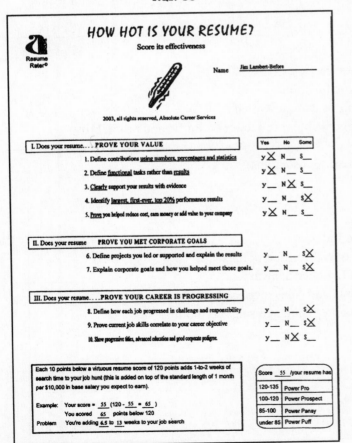

AFTER

RQI: 130

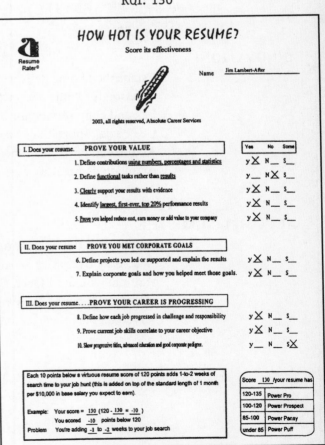

JIM LAMBERT

2434 Bestview Lane
La Grange, IL, 60513
(773) 239-2768

OBJECTIVE: I am seeking a position where my 21 years of sales, marketing, and management experience can be utilized to increase market share and company profits while pursuing new opportunities for career challenges with a company who places high priority on customer satisfaction, initiative and quality performance.

EXPERIENCE: OWNER AND CORPORATE PRESIDENT
Convenient Food Mart Franchise, 1977–1999

Owned and operated a grocery store franchise. Accountable for all aspects of business operations. Sales in excess of $30,000 weekly. Developed weekly and monthly work plans based upon projected sales. Coordinated aggressive and creative merchandising plans to achieve maximum sales. Purchased inventory, which included adjusting product mix, space allocation, stock levels, new product development, and customer research. Created pricing strategies to maximize profit margins while being aware of customer expectations and satisfaction. Responsible for support staff human resource functions including developing personnel policies, job posting, interviewing, hiring, training, and scheduling.

INNOVATION:

- Established home delivery service.
- Catering for home and business functions.
- Fax and copy service for business and individuals.
- US. Postal Substation. Major contributor to increased traffic and profitability
- Automated teller machine.
- Active in community events and sponsorships

ACCOMPLISHMENTS:

- First million dollar location in Indiana.
- 17 consecutive years of sales over 1 million dollars.
- Multiple winner of Operation Excellence award.
- Multiple winner of sales volume and sales increase awards
- Served on parent corporation advertising and sales committee.

OWNER AND TREASURER
Spring Pop Beverage Bottling, 1985–1989

Owned and operated an independent bottling company. Accountable for all aspects of multi-million dollar business operations. Enhanced existing manufacturing facilities to include a retail sales environment. Grew business by expanding product line and merchandise mix. Managed production, including purchasing, inventory control and distribution to retail and wholesale accounts. Developed weekly and monthly work plans based upon production projections.

INNOVATION:

- Built external sales by securing private label bottling contracts with individual businesses.
- Developed a wholesale sales operation through customer cold calling.
- Enhanced brand awareness throughout the community by organizing and leading tours of the production facilities for schools and youth groups.
- Commissioned and worked with a printer to redesign product labels and artwork.
- Interviewed, hired, and trained sales force.
- Worked with sales force to establish and maintain proper customer protocols.
- Performed research and analysis for business decisions related to capital expenditure for new equipment.

EDUCATION:

Northwestern, Chicago, IL 1977
Bachelor of Science in Marketing
Bachelor of Science in Management

CONTINUING
EDUCATION: Global Knowledge—Understanding Computer Networks Knowledgeable in Quicken and Microsoft Office products including Word, Outlook, and Excel.

JIM LAMBERT

34 Bestview, La Grange, IL, 60513 773-239-2768, Email Jim256@aol.com

OBJECTIVE   Sales, business development, marketing, or operations management: an opportunity to streamline operations, execute business plans, cut costs, increase profits, and improve staff performance.

· SUMMARY ·

I've built two businesses, a franchise that hit numerous sales/volume records and a beverage bottling operation that produced $1,200,000 annually. Success is a result of managing complex business functions, simplifying processes to improve efficiency, and managing relations with staff and customers.

EXPERIENCE

1980–1999   **General Manager/Partner** _____ *Convenient Food Mart Franchise*
Overview   Grew sales **550%, from $288,000/yr to $1,600,000/yr,** by initiating quality standards and cost controls, and executing creative merchandising programs. We ranked in the top 5% (out of 96,700 convenient stores) based on average sales per sq ft and gross volume as noted in the 1999 *Convenience Store News* statistical report.

Challenge   Originally paid $50K for an underperforming franchise that lacked marketing and positive community public relations; hence, it was ranked #50 of 100 Indiana franchises. Within four years, I created the #1 ranked franchise based on sales and became the first in Indiana to break the $1,000,000 sales plateau.
Innovations: introduced home delivery, ATMs, and a US Postal substation, which doubled daily foot traffic.

Results   Ranked #1 store of 100 Indiana properties for 12 of 17 years.
Won 6 Operation Excellence and 8 sales volume/sales increase awards.
First million dollar location in Illinois; 17 consecutive years of sales $1,000,000+.
Received recognition letters from franchiser for excellence in Meeting Corporate Standards.

Actions
- *Operations* .... Developed work plans based upon projected sales, purchasing needs, and schedule of 15 staff.
- *Training*   .... Coached employees to ensure service quality generated customer loyalty and repeat business.
- *Budgeting* .... Maintained costs to attain an average store operating profit of 20%.
- *Promotions*.......... Created seasonal themes, discounts, special promotions, and monthly direct mail campaigns. Served on parent corporation's advertising and sales committee.
- *P.R.* .... Active Community Relations: sponsored 12 sport teams and donated to schools or local churches.

1985–1989   *Owner/Treasurer* _____ *Spring Pop Beverage Bottling*
Overview   Purchased and ran a $1.2MM bottling company that I added wholesale distribution to existing retail sales.

Challenge   The wholesale channel became possible after investing $70,000 for new technology to extend the product line and by developing bottling contracts with outside businesses. I enhanced brand awareness in the community by leading tours of the production facilities, by cold-calling retailers, and by marketing the unique characteristics of a 60-year-old Chicago gourmet soda manufacturer.

Innovations   Research determined capital expenditure for new equipment (added plastic to the existing glass bottling capability). Created new price and quantity discount programs to induce grocery chains to stock our product.

EDUCATION   Dual Degree, B.S., Marketing & B.S., Management   Northwestern, Chicago, IL

JIM LAMBERT'S STORY

Success Snapshot: Jim landed a career at UBS PaineWebber, a transition from owning a convenience store.

Career Sweet Spot: Jim's job is in the primary field he wanted to explore, investment consulting, even though he had no previous professional experience and was over fifty years old.

Trouble Spot Fixed: A twenty-two-year career as the co-owner of a Convenience Food Mart franchise, meaning he had a narrow career path.

To Use This Chart:
1. Score your resume.
2. Find Before and After RQI scores in the PYV, MCG, and CPS categories similar to your scores.
3. Strengthen your weaknesses using our tactics.

BEFORE SCORE			of 100%	Score
Category I	Prove Your Value	PYV = 46%		30 of 75
Category II	Met Corporate Goals	MCG = 33%		10 of 30
Category III	Career Progress Status	CPS = 50%		15 of 30
Their RQI Score:			**44%**	**55 of 135**

AFTER SCORE			of 100%	Score
Category I	Prove Your Value	PYV = 100%		75 of 75
Category II	Met Corporate Goals	MCG = 100%		30 of 30
Category III	Career Progress Status	CPS = 83%		25 of 30
Our RQI Score:			**96%**	**130 of 135**

CAREER STATS

Career Field:	Financial Consulting
Old Title:	Franchise Owner
New Title:	Financial Consultant
Bridge or Ladder:	Bridge

IMPROVEMENT

From:	Power Puff
To:	Power Pro

KEY

Power Pro:	95% RQI	Power Pansy:	60–80% RQI
Power Prospect:	80–95% RQI	Power Puff:	Below 60% RQI

RICHARD ALTMAN

Unemployed PE Teacher

CAREER HIGHLIGHTS

- Salary increase with his new resume: $55,000 (went from unemployed)

- Promoted to full-time teacher

- Job search length: one summer

BEFORE

RQI: 30

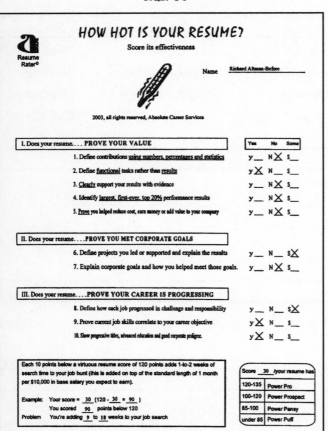

AFTER

RQI: 105

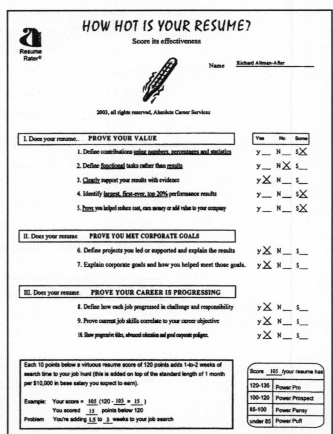

Richard Altman
1555 Trenton Way
Madison, WI 53515
608-295-3889

OBJECTIVE   To obtain a teaching position in the areas of physical education and/or drivers' education

EMPLOYMENT

Physical Education Teacher
SPECIAL EDUCATION DISTRICT OF DANE COUNTY   1991–Present
    Responsible for:
- Planning and implementing a Physical Education program for 120 B.D. students
- Coaching and refereeing athletic events
- Improving curriculum and developing programs that utilize community facilities
- Maintaining facilities and equipment
- Participating in evaluation of students and developing I.E.P. goals and objectives
- Facilitating participation in Alternative High School Athletic League
- Developing and implementing an intramural program
- Applying for and receiving a grant for Outdoor Education
- Participating on Re-entry Committee for the determination of main streaming students

Physical Education and Drivers' Education Teacher
EAST HIGH SCHOOL   1987–1991
    Responsibilities and accomplishments:
- Implementing drivers' education curriculum which employed a variety of instructional techniques designed to deal with students with a range of academic skills and severe behavior disorders
- Monitoring students' academic performance and progress
- Coordinating schedules of students and other staff

Head Coach—Girls' Track
Assistant Coach—Boy's Track
EAST HIGH SCHOOL   1989–1992
- Coached Team to Conference Championship 1991
- Coached State Qualifiers

Drivers' Education Teacher
MIDDLETON HIGH SCHOOL   1986–1987

Physical Education Teacher
COTTAGE GROVE HIGH SCHOOL   1985–1986
- Coached Volleyball and Basketball
- Organized and directed all-school "Olympic Day"

Richard Altman

Assistant Coach—Boys' Football and Wrestling
MEMORIAL HIGH SCHOOL   1981–1985

Sixth Grad. Teacher/Lead Teacher
GOMPERS MIDDLE SCHOOL   1983–1984

Responsible for:
- Planning and instructing eights subject areas
- Planning and instructing science curriculum as lead teacher

Supervisor
AIR COURIER DISPATCH   1979–1981

EDUCATION

Bachelor of Arts in Physical Education
UNIVERSITY OF ILLINOIS AT CHICAGO

SKILLS

- Adept at handling numerous tasks simultaneously
- Respected reputation for fairness in dealing with students, parents, and staff
- Proven background in establishing **new** programs
- Certified in Non-Violent Crisis Intervention

RICHARD ALTMAN
1555 Trenton Way Madison, WI 53515, 608-295-3889

TEACHING EXPERIENCE

2001-present	**Teacher** - Physical Education	DISTRICT 75 Shorewood Elementary

Co-teach with two other educators a total of 650 students K-8. The key focus is to implement a full elementary and junior high curriculum within a bilingual fully mainstreamed classroom environment.

1991-2001	**Teacher** - Physical Education	SPECIAL EDUCATION DISTRICT OF DANE COUNTY

Taught 9 PE classed to 120 students a day. Created lesson plans, intramural programs and special events to gain State of Illinois teaching goals. Implemented the following strategies to optimize student's ability to learn.

Teaching   *Goal 1*   • *Effective communication skills*
Strategy   Use group discussions on topics tied to a recent activity within a talking circle where each student communicates without interference.
Benefit   *For the student*   They learn to respect personal opinions, reduce their tendency to remain isolated and accept unique cultural distinctions without discrimination.

Teaching   *Goal 2*   • *The process of making decisions*
Strategy   Rotate students through leadership roles i.e.: team Captains, Referees and Coaches.
Benefit   *For the student*   Leadership roles reveal both the obvious and hidden talents and they learn the impact of their decisions on fellow classmates.

Teaching   *Goal 3*   • *How to contribute and thrive on teams*
Strategy   Use ice breakers, problem solving, trust building, and deinhibitizing activities as tactics to foster team environments and debriefing strategies to process and summarize the lesson value.
Benefit   *For the student*   They learn to cooperate, appreciate peer's contributions and work together.

Teaching   *Goal 4*   • *The benefits of lifelong exercise and nutrition management*
Strategy   Present the underlying scientific facts to prove the concepts are sound and convincing so that students modify their behavior and journalize a history of their actions.
Benefit   *For the student*   Reduced stress, improved mental health and balance life.

Project   In 1996, I received a $2000 grant from the SEDOL foundation to take students to Iron Oaks Adventure Center.
Results: Rolled Adventure Education and Challenge Education techniques into each of my teaching goals.

Project   Enhancing overall programming and value of SEDOL Physical Education Program. **Results** - implemented the first Bowling unit at community facilities and the first Frisbee Golf unit using a park district gold course. Coordinated first school-wide volleyball tournaments and developed 3-on-3 basketball tournament.

DRIVERS EDUCATION TEACHING EXPERIENCE

1987-1991	**Teacher-P.E. & Drivers Education**	EAST HIGH SCHOOL
1986-1987	**Drivers Education Teacher**	MIDDLETON HIGH SCHOOL

Need   Engaging students into the learning process while ensuring they attain the lesson objectives.

Methods   • *Role Playing*   used to address drinking & driving, road rage, and how emotions influence our driving patterns.

   • *Mental Gymnastics*   used to visualize, anticipate and respond to mundane or hazardous driving scenarios.

   • *Behavior Modification*   reveal student's true behavior patterns which are then discussed relative to national statistics.

Benefits   Creates an environment where student participation and learning is greatly enhanced.

Education   BA, Physical Education   University of Illinois at Chicago

RICHARD ALTMAN'S STORY

Success Snapshot: Richard was fired by his school principal, who would not give him a good recommendation. A catastrophic situation for a teacher with a long-term position. After I illustrated his contributions, he accepted two job offers before the next school year started.

Career Sweet Spot: Richard was hired by two different schools that allowed him to work for them concurrently.

Trouble Spot Fixed: Overcame a negative reference and allowed him to land a new teaching role without an employment gap.

To Use This Chart:
1. Score your resume.
2. Find Before and After RQI scores in the PYV, MCG, and CPS categories similar to your scores.
3. Strengthen your weaknesses using our tactics.

BEFORE SCORE				of 100%	Score
Category I	Prove Your Value	PYV	=	0%	0 of 75
Category II	Met Corporate Goals	MCG	=	17%	5 of 30
Category III	Career Progress Status	CPS	=	83%	25 of 30
	Their RQI Score:			**22%**	**30 of 135**

AFTER SCORE				of 100%	Score
Category I	Prove Your Value	PYV	=	73%	55 of 75
Category II	Met Corporate Goals	MCG	=	66%	20 of 30
Category III	Career Progress Status	CPS	=	100%	30 of 30
	Our RQI Score:			**78%**	**105 of 135**

CAREER STATS

Career Field:	Education
Old Title:	PE Teacher
New Title:	PE Teacher
Bridge or Ladder:	Reemployed

IMPROVEMENT

From:	Power Puff
To:	Power Pansy

KEY

Power Pro:	95% RQI	Power Pansy:	60–80% RQI
Power Prospect:	80–95% RQI	Power Puff:	Below 60% RQI

DANIEL WALLACE

Technology to Politics

CAREER HIGHLIGHTS

- Salary increase with his new resume: $10,000

- Promoted to systems administrator and secretary of correspondence for a US senator

- Job search length: six weeks

BEFORE

RQI: 20

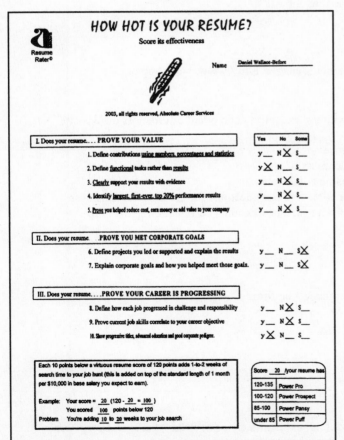

AFTER

RQI: 135

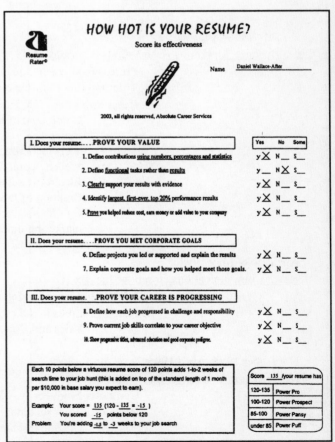

DANIEL WALLACE

1326 Sandy Ave, Lagrange, IL 60529

708-229-3865   dawall@yahoo.com

Work Experience

July 1998–Present 2001

Northwestern Medical Center—Chicago. IL

Center For Advanced Technology and International Health
Title: Director, Special Projects
Responsibilities include:
- Middle East Liaison for the Center's regional office in Abu Dhabi, United Arab Emirates
- Coordinate all support, logistics and protocol for visiting dignitaries
- Support CEO, Gary Mechlenburg MD, with all special projects
- Support the Telemedicine Program
- Create new programs to utilize resources within the organization to broaden our market domestically and internationally

Northwestern Health Services
Title: Marketing Coordinator
Responsibilities include:
- Copywriting, event planning, event promotion, international conduct guidelines (protocol education), international communication, ambassadorial functions for VIP's

July 1998–August 1999

Business Marketing Association—Chicago. IL

Professional Association Internet Manager: http://www.marketing.org
Title: Internet Coordinator
Responsibilities include:
- Communication with top executives and board of directors on Website issues
- Website maintenance
- Website communications
- Electronic advertising consultations
- Creation of Information Age test questions for the Certified Business Communicator (CBC) test, a professional certification in the B2B marketing industry

April 1996–May 1998

Hawk Communications Group—Chicago. IL

Founding member of Internet marketing firm.
Responsibilities include:
- Sales and Consulting

November 1995–April 1996

MicroRepair Associates. Inc.—Chicago. IL

Computer Engineer
Responsibilities include:
- On-Site troubleshooting and maintenance of PC's, Mac's, and peripherals

Education

<u>1999</u>	Columbia College, B.A. (concentration in Marketing Communications/PR) 3.9 GPA
<u>94–95</u>	University of Arizona, Tucson.
	Major: Political Science (concentration in Political Theory)
<u>92–94</u>	University of Vermont, Burlington. Major: Political Science
	(concentration in International Relations and Political Theory)
	Minor: Speech and Rhetoric (concentration in Argumentation and Logic/Reason)
<u>1992</u>	Francis Parker High School, Chicago, IL

Skills

<u>Computer/Internet</u>

- Founding member of Hawk Communications Group (acquired by Cramer Technical Services Q2 98), an Internet marketing firm specializing in consulting, the creation of Web sites, and the publication of beneficial information to the Internet community.
- Notable Site Directions: www.hawkweb.com, "In Memoriam: Cardinal Bernadin" (with Archdiocese of Chicago), "In Memoriam: Deng Xiao Ping," www.bluesbeforesunrise.com, and various independent groups
- Direction Consultation on: www.ochsnerusa.com, www.lickbike.com
- Working knowledge of Photoshop, HTML (Web Language, non-asssited), and computer hardware

<u>Human Resources</u>

- Trained in Mediation Conflict Resolution
- Attended four invitational leadership training seminars

<u>Public Speaking</u>

- Invited to speak at the School of the Art Institute of Chicago on Internet architecture, Web site direction, and Web site

DANIEL WALLACE

1326 Sandy Ave   La Grange, IL 60529 • 708-229-3865 • danwallace@yahoo.com

| 7/98–Present | **N O R T H W E S T E R N   M E D I C A L   C E N T E R** | Chicago, IL |

| | 8/99–now | **Director, Special Projects** | *Advanced Technology—International Health*   (ATIH) |
| | 7/98–8/99 | **Marketing Coordinator** | *Northwestern International Health Services* |

Overview.............. 8/99–now **Director special projects** came after I built the ATIH website and was invited onto the team by the hospital's CEO, Gary Mechlenburg.

Strategies to build business include identifying political, royal, and business leaders across the globe with whom we network. I also write white papers that highlight health care technologies (i.e., telemedicine) and products that apply to both developing countries and U.S. markets.

Actions ⇨ Middle East liaison for the center's regional office in United Arab Emirates

⇨ Coordinate all support, logistics, and protocol for visiting dignitaries

⇨ Plan events and oversee meetings with foreign health ministers

Result — Authored a technology and health care report given to the heads of state of the 15 ECOWAS nations and used by the previous White House administration during the president's trip to Nigeria in 2000.

Overview.............. 7/98–8/99 As **marketing coordinator**, I helped Northwestern increase the international patient base by marketing the department to create a buzz among the hospital's 1,033 doctors who could generate referrals.

Actions ⇨ Deployed an awareness campaign with the 1,033 Northwestern doctors

⇨ Executed a targeted marketing strategy delivered to 250 Chicago hotels

⇨ Built recognition for Northwestern at 184 D.C.-based embassies

Results — Increased revenues and patient load by 100% within two years.

Unique Created the first public speaking event at Northwestern Medical Center for the Dalai Lama's personal physician, Dr. Tenzin Choedrak. The event succeeded by executing a marketing strategy whereby we motivated traditional medical practitioners by promoting the Dalai Lama's alternative medical practices.

7/98–8/99 **Internet Manager,** Chicago, IL   **BUSINESS MARKETING ASSOCIATION**
Overview.............. Recruited by the executive director with the mandate of enhancing their Internet presence.

Challenge This was a manpower and operational efficiency objective tied to a technology solution, whereby I enhanced the website by creating strategies to respond to member inquiries, problems, and program needs, which freed up the 3 staff who managed the association day-to-day.

Actions ⇨ Created a new member auto responder

⇨ Created a training resource site with available B2B seminars and conferences

⇨ Revitalized a stagnant job bank that became a well-trafficked site feature

⇨ Consulted with executives and corporate boards on web advertising strategies

Results —— Enhancements nearly eliminated the staff's need to respond to mundane inquiries and greatly improved member satisfaction.

| 4/96–5/98 | **Founding Member** | **HAWK COMMUNICATIONS GROUP,** Chicago, IL |

(acquired by Cramer Technical Services Q2—1998)

Overview.............. Internet marketing consulting firm, website creator and publisher of Internet community information.

EDUCATION   5/99   Columbia College, B.A., concentration in marketing communications/PR
3.9 GPA

TRAINING   Mediation Conflict Resolution   Attended 4 invitational leadership training seminars

TECHNICAL   Photoshop   MS Office   HTML (Web Language, non-assisted)

LANGUAGES   French, Basic German, Russian, and Japanese. Currently studying Italian.

ACHIEVEMENTS Invited to judge Internet marketing projects for the ProComm Awards, the international business-to-business advertising competition, by the Business Marketing Association.

Invited to judge electronic media categories for the Insurance Marketing Communication Awards. Judged websites, TV & radio commercials, and various Internet supportive endeavors.

Guest speaker, Internet architecture, School of the Art Institute of Chicago

Invited to two separate Prince William County, VA, leadership conferences
Invited to two separate Hugh O'Brien Foundation leadership conferences

Harvard University Book Prize

PERSONAL   Board member—The Illinois Medical District Guest House Foundation
Board member—Wallace Charitable Trust
Affiliations: Jobs for Youth and AidsCare

DAN WALLACE'S STORY

Success Snapshot: Dan desired to work in politics. His new resume led to a job as systems administrator and correspondence secretary for a senator in Oregon.

Career Sweet Spot: At twenty-five years old, six weeks after starting a job search, he got into politics.

Trouble Spot Fixed: Overcame a complete lack of political experience and was hired in a rare role—only 100 US senators exist.

To Use This Chart:
1. Score your resume.
2. Find Before and After RQI scores in the PYV, MCG, and CPS categories similar to your scores.
3. Strengthen your weaknesses using our tactics.

BEFORE SCORE				**of 100%**	**Score**
Category I	Prove Your Value	PYV	=	0%	0 of 75
Category II	Met Corporate Goals	MCG	=	33%	10 of 30
Category III	Career Progress Status	CPS	=	33%	10 of 30
	Their RQI Score:			15%	**20 of 135**

AFTER SCORE				**of 100%**	**Score**
Category I	Prove Your Value	PYV	= 100%		75 of 75
Category II	Met Corporate Goals	MCG	= 100%		30 of 30
Category III	Career Progress Status	CPS	= 100%		30 of 30
	Our RQI Score:			100%	**135 of 135**

CAREER STATS

Career Field:	Technology
Old Title:	Dir. Special Projects
New Title:	Systems Administrator
Bridge or Ladder:	Bridge

IMPROVEMENT

From:	Power Puff
To:	Power Pro

KEY

Power Pro:	95% RQI	Power Pansy:	60–80% RQI
Power Prospect:	80–95% RQI	Power Puff:	Below 60% RQI

ABBY HARRINGTON

Nonprofit Manager

CAREER HIGHLIGHTS

• Salary increase with her new resume: $20,000

• Promoted to C.O.O.

• Job search length: ten weeks

BEFORE

RQI: 50

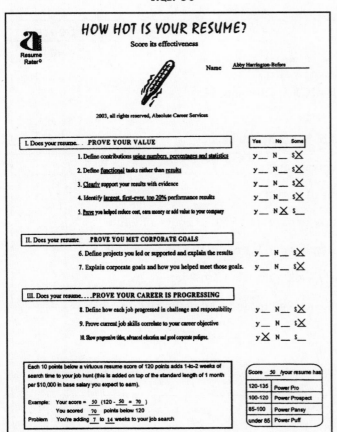

AFTER

RQI: 135

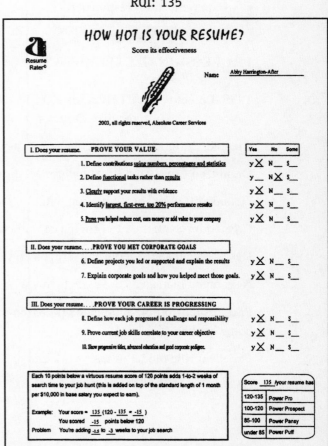

ABBY HARRINGTON
1370 Clarence St.
Forest Park, IL 60130
708-339-6878

SUMMARY

Experienced non-profit director with a track record of accomplishments in development, organization and administration of start-up and special projects in health and human services. Strong background in systems design and organizational dynamics. Innovative leader; capable of conceptualizing and implementing new business ventures. Able to build relationships and networks. Proven success in leading organizations through change, and commitment to team work.

- Excellent organizational skills, establishes realistic priorities moves with deliberateness.
- Successful administrator in planning, organizing and directing work; effective use of interpersonal, communication and listening skills.
- Proven ability in finding creative, innovative solutions to complex problems with commitment to quality.
- Diverse experience in health care settings.
- Experienced Pit responsibility

PROFESSIONAL EXPERIENCE

1995–Present **LUTHERAN SOCIAL SERVICES, Chicago, IL**
Executive Director

Created, designed and implemented all aspects of home health agency

Organized Corporate Structures for Medicare/private duty

Obtained JCAHO accreditation within 6 months of start-up

Created infrastructure to provide care in currently in excess of 16,000 hours a month

Designed/enhanced reporting structures; total number current of employees over 350.

Negotiated managed care agreements with HMO's and physician provider groups

P&L responsibility; anticipated/prepared for balanced budget act and its impact on home health

Excellent role model of teamwork and dedication

Abby Harrington

1993–1995   **Lutheran Social Services,** Chicago, IL
External Coordinator

Designed/implemented overall external strategy

Set direction, goals, and implementation for major gift program

Implemented speakers bureau throughout archdiocese

Organized/managed archdiocesan volunteer program

Designed and implemented matching gift program

1990–1993   **Center for Development in Ministry (CDM),** Chicago, IL
Assistant Director

Created and implemented marketing and development activities

Redesigned existing booking systems

Managed and redefined financial systems

Coordinated special projects

1989–1990   **Re-Generating Lutheran Faith**, Chicago, IL
Project Director

Directed an 18-month national project designed to bring young adults back into the Lutheran Church.

Managed and coordinated national steering committee

Obtained funding from foundations

Maintained fiscal responsibility, with fiduciary capacity to foundations

Developed national database

Planned meeting/special events leading up to 3-day symposium in 1990; coordinated symposium video

Organized/implemented all aspects of public relations

Maintained and managed volunteer staff

Coordinated special events and dinner/speaker series *for* Crossroads Center for Faith and Work

Abby Harrington

1975–1980   **Lake Forest Estates Primary Care Physicians**, Lake Forest, IL
Administrator

Developed, organized and implemented administration of medical practice handling 14,000 patients

Responsible for total administrative operation

P&L responsibility

Assisted in formulation of strategic plans

1985   **Assurance Care Associates**, Lake Forest, IL
Executive Director

Coordinated corporate and organizational structure for 47 member WA group

Organized financial structures

Identified and budgeting of short-term financial needs

Secured managed care contracts

1974–1975   **East Memorial Hospital**, Milwaukee, WI
Associate Director, Operating Room

Coordinated daily functions of operating and recovery room Designed and taught cardiology program for nurses

1970 –1973   **St. Francis Hospital**, Milwaukee, IL
Registered Nurse

Open-heart unit staff nurse

EDUCATION
Depaul University	MBA	January 1999
University of Wisconsin, Milwaukee		1971
St. Xavier Hospital School of Nursing	RN	1970

ABBY HARRINGTON
1370 Clarence St., Forest Park, IL   60130 708-339-6878

OBJECTIVE

To continue using leadership abilities in organizational development, business planning, operational analysis, and systematic design of programs to attain financial targets and mission objectives.

EXPERIENCE
1989–present

Overview

LUTHERAN SOCIAL SERVICES, Chicago, IL
Executive Director—Lutheran Home Care   **1995–present**
While holding concurrent title of director of nursing and starting an MBA program, I created Lutheran Social Services' *first home health agency.* The agency now has *350+ employees* handling 9,000 Medicare visits annually and providing *16,000 hours per month* of managed care, private duty, and state-funded CCP programs. Revenues have increased to current income of *$2,800,000* annually and is tracking to gross *$3,200,000* by FY 99.

Actions
- Reorganized an inefficient program to cut $127K loss. This restructuring provided the cash flow necessary to fund the home health care program.
- Secured on first application: Licensure with the IL Dept. of Public Health (IDPH).
- Organized corporate structure (501C3).
- Handled P/L responsibilities to ensure compliance with the balanced budget act.
- Awarded HCFA Medicare certification.
- Created manual to secure JCAHO accreditation within 6 months of incorporating.
- Negotiated 3 HMO and physician provider group contracts tracking at $700K.

Keys
The challenge was creating a home health care program within a social service agency tied to a religious denomination. Success is a result of (1) completing all accreditation pro forma in 6 months, (2) developing systematic structures to support health care programs, (3) hiring and educating employees to win their support for mission objectives.

Overview

Director of Annual Fundraising Campaign, Lutheran Social Services   **1993–1995**
Designed and implemented strategies to create the *Major Donor Program* for individual contributors who gave more than $5,000. Results increased funds 33% in a year (from $665,000 to $1,000,000+).

Actions
- Implemented speakers' bureau throughout archdiocese
- Organized/managed volunteer program (100+ participants)
- Designed and implemented matching gift program

Keys
The primary challenge was to (1) identify major donors from 377 parishes; (2) after creating a database of 150 donors, I then built close relationships and used special events to solidify their ongoing support.

Overview

Assistant Director, Conference Center for Lutheran Brotherhood   **1990–1993**

Reorganized event planning and promotional efforts for conference center. Within 3 years we doubled attendees from 16,000 to 32,000 and grew revenues from $600,000 to $1,050,000.

Actions
- Implemented marketing plans and redesigned existing booking systems.
- Managed and redefined financial systems.
- Coordinated special projects.

Keys   The challenge was to (1) evaluate existing processes related to event booking and (2) identify efficiencies that could be implemented; (3) the final phase was to recreate marketing literature and conduct direct marketing to existing customer base to generate awareness.

Overview

Project Director, Regenerating Lutheran Faith   **1989–1990**

Directed 18-month national project to bring young adults back into the Lutheran Church.

Actions
- Managed and coordinated national steering committee.
- Helped obtain foundation funding of $100,000.
- Maintained fiscal responsibility and fiduciary accountability to foundations.
- Developed national database with 7,000 contacts.
- Planned special events and 3-day national symposium with 220 attendees.
- Directed P.R. and coordinated speaker series.

1975–1988

LAKE FOREST ESTATES PRIMARY CARE PHYSICIANS, Lake Forest, IL
Administrator Manager

Overview

When first hired, the practice consisted of 1 doctor seeing an average of 150 patients per week. Within 8 years I helped grow the practice to encompass 3 clinics with 11 doctors and a staff of 50 employees with total revenues of **$2,000,000–$2,500,000** annually.

Actions   Implemented administration of medical practice handling 14,000 patients. Responsible for total administrative operation. P/L responsibility.

1974–1975

ASSURANCE CARE ASSOCIATES, Lake Forest, IL
Executive Director

Overview

Recruited by a group of 4 doctors to create Assurance Care Associates. Identified liability issues and assessed financial funding needs for startup and organizational structure to support 47-member IPA. Within a year we secured managed care contracts.

Actions   Coordinated corporate, financial, and organizational structure for 47-member IPA group. Identified and budgeted short-term financial needs.

EDUCATION
1/99

MBA, DePaul University
RN, St. Xavier Hospital School of Nursing

ABBY HARRINGTON'S STORY

Success Snapshot: Abby wanted to convert her MBA into a more challenging career role. Her new resume helped her become chief operating officer of a large Safety Foundation.

Career Sweet Spot: As the COO, she impacts the vision and corporate direction of the entire organization.

Trouble Spot Fixed: Overcame a narrow, institutionalized career path of working for a religious denomination. In itself, this is not a problem, but she felt constrained.

To Use This Chart:
1. Score your resume.
2. Find Before and After RQI scores in the PYV, MCG, and CPS categories similar to your scores.
3. Strengthen your weaknesses using our tactics.

BEFORE SCORE			**of 100%**	**Score**
Category I	Prove Your Value	PYV = 27%		20 of 75
Category II	Met Corporate Goals	MCG = 33%		10 of 30
Category III	Career Progress Status	CPS = 67%		20 of 30
	Their RQI Score:		37%	**50 of 135**

AFTER SCORE			**of 100%**	**Score**
Category I	Prove Your Value	PYV = 100%		75 of 75
Category II	Met Corporate Goals	MCG = 100%		30 of 30
Category III	Career Progress Status	CPS = 100%		30 of 30
	Our RQI Score:		100%	**135 of 135**

CAREER STATS

Career Field:	Health Care
Old Title:	Director
New Title:	COO
Bridge or Ladder:	Ladder

IMPROVEMENT

From:	Power Puff
To:	Power Pro

KEY

Power Pro:	95% RQI	Power Pansy:	60–80% RQI
Power Prospect:	80–95% RQI	Power Puff:	Below 60% RQI

PAUL BENDER

Retail to Technology

CAREER HIGHLIGHTS

- Salary increase with his new resume: $49,000

- Promoted from retail sales clerk to network administrator

- Job search length: seamless

<table>
<tr><th>BEFORE</th><th>AFTER</th></tr>
<tr><td>RQI: 15</td><td>RQI: 125</td></tr>
</table>

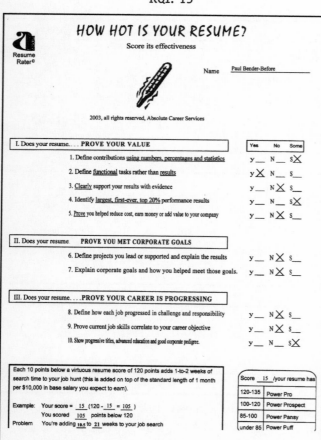

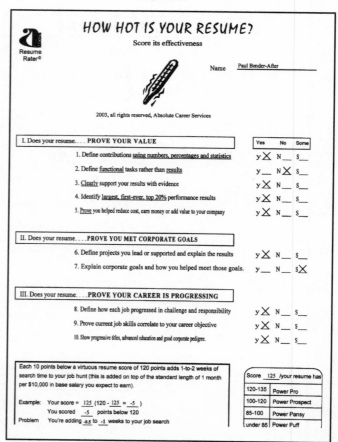

PAUL P. BENDER

138 Monroe St. Charleston, SC 20401   ☏ 843- 312-5879

Employment

October, 1995 To Present	Circuit City Stores, Inc. Sales Counselor	Charleston, SC

- Assisted customers with the purchase of home electronics in a fast paced and fully commissioned sales environment.
- Licensed to design and sell home and car audio systems, home and car security systems, program and activate cellular phones, as well as other electronics.
- Attended numerous training seminars and product knowledge and sales technique, sponsored by Circuit City and their vendors.
- Was given Exceptional Customer Service award from corporate office in February 1996. Was also awarded "Presidents Club" for being in top 25% of sales force nation wide.

June, 1994 to October, 1995	Circuit City Stores, Inc. Customer Service Associate	Charleston, SC

- Provided all types of post-purchase support for customers.
- Emphasized resolving problems with product use and function.
- Processed credit applications for four independent finance companies.
- Screened incoming applicants for employment eligibility. Often conducted preliminary interviews to assist management.
- Processes returns, services, and special orders for the store.

May, 1993 to June, 1994	Black's Tire Co.	Myrtle Beach, SC

- Responsible for mounting & dismounting& balancing & and repairing car and truck tires.
- Operated various types of heavy machinery including high pressure jacks and "zip guns" for use on full size trucks.
- Worked with customers on special requests or complaints to ensure total customer satisfaction.

EDUCATION	Morton College (Currently enrolled) Business major

PAUL P. BENDER

138 Monroe St. Charleston, SC 29401   ☎ 843-312-5879

OBJECTIVE

To continue a successful sales career as an account executive for a company that will use my ability to assess needs, develop client partnerships, and the necessary diligence to attain budgeted goals.

SUMMARY

Professional Qualifications in sales and merchandising. Use organizational and interpersonal communication skills to maintain productive working relationships with management, staff employees, and the general public.

Personal Emphasis is to provide operational support to managers and to maintain high standards by focusing on a detailed, organized, and result-oriented performance approach.

EMPLOYMENT
6/94–Present

SALES COUNSELOR, **CIRCUIT CITY STORES, INC.** Charleston, SC

▫ Assist customer purchases of home electronics in a fast-paced and fully commissioned sales environment.

RESULTS

Achieved monthly volume budget of $16,000–$30,000 and profit margin budget of 26% (working part-time).
Average sale is $600, which is 200%–300% better than the per-sale store average.

▫ Design and sell packaged systems, accessories, installation services, and extended warranties for a product selection mix of over 1,200 items including:
• Home Audio • Car Audio   • Security Systems   • Portable Electronics

▫ Attended vendor-sponsored training, product knowledge, and sales technique seminars.

▫ Qualify customers on their perceived needs and financial constraints to determine expectations and create a "best fit" sale.

RECOGNITION

Awarded Exceptional Customer Service award from corporate office in 1996.
Awarded "Presidents Club" for being in top 25% of sales force nationwide 1996.

CUSTOMER SERVICE ASSOCIATE   6/94–10/95
▫ Provided post-purchase support for customers, resolved complaints, processed returns and special orders.

▫ Processed credit applications for four independent finance companies.

▫ Screened incoming applicants for employment eligibility and conducted preliminary interviews to assist management with staff selection.

5/93–6/94

MECHANICAL ASSISTANT, **BLACKS TIRE CO.,** Myrtle Beach, SC
▫ Operated heavy machinery, including high pressure jacks and "zip guns."

▫ Worked with customers on special requests or complaints to ensure total satisfaction.

EDUCATION

Present, Charleston College—Business Major

COMPUTER

Applications: Harvard Graphics, WordPerfect, Windows, Lotus.

AVAILABLE REFERENCES ON REQUEST

PAUL BENDER'S STORY

Success Snapshot: Helped a Circuit City sales clerk break into the IT field. Three jobs later, he worked for Morning Star Financial, a global investment research firm. His earnings increased from $16,000 to $65,000 a year—without a college degree and before he turned twenty-seven.

Career Sweet Spot: Elevated a retail sales clerk to a solid technology role as systems administrator.

Trouble Spot Fixed: He had a dead-end retail sales career, no college degree, and felt his life was stagnating.

To Use This Chart:
1. Score your resume.
2. Find Before and After RQI scores in the PYV, MCG, and CPS categories similar to your scores.
3. Strengthen your weaknesses using our tactics.

BEFORE SCORE			of 100%	Score
Category I	Prove Your Value	PYV = 13%		10 of 75
Category II	Met Corporate Goals	MCG = 0%		0 of 30
Category III	Career Progress Status	CPS = 17%		5 of 30
	Their RQI Score:		11%	**15 of 135**

AFTER SCORE			of 100%	Score
Category I	Prove Your Value	PYV = 100%		75 of 75
Category II	Met Corporate Goals	MCG = 67%		20 of 30
Category III	Career Progress Status	CPS = 100%		30 of 30
	Our RQI Score:		93%	**125 of 135**

CAREER STATS

Career Field:	Technology
Old Title:	Circuit City Sales
New Title:	Network Admin.
Bridge or Ladder:	Bridge and Ladder

IMPROVEMENT

From:	Power Puff
To:	Power Prospect

KEY

Power Pro:	95% RQI	Power Pansy:	60–80% RQI
Power Prospect:	80–95% RQI	Power Puff:	Below 60% RQI

ELISE HANSON

Change to Pharmaceutical Sales from Printing

CAREER HIGHLIGHTS

- Salary increase with her new resume: $45,000

- Promoted to inside sales at pharmaceutical company, Merck & Co. Then became territory sales manager at Baxter Healthcare.

BEFORE

RQI: 55

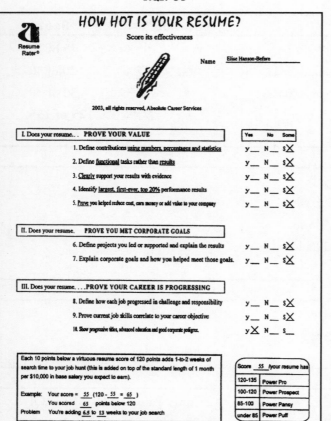

AFTER

RQI: 135

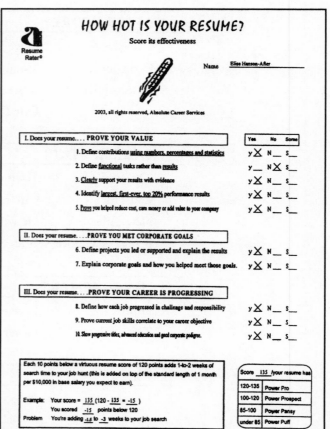

ELISE HANSON

4982 Madison St.
Minneapolis, MN 55401
612-698-2840

April 1994 — Present   **Rampage Graphics. Inc. Minneapolis, Minnesota**

Rampage Graphics is a two million dollar, privately held, graphic finishing company. It provides the printing and advertising industry with foil stamped, embossed, and die-cut finished commercial products.

- Served 4 years as sales representative to the Illinois, Iowa, and Minnesota markets
- 3 years as sales manager
- 1 year as Sales Director and CEO

Sales Rep:
- Outside sales representative responsible for development of new business accounts and developing existing relationships.
- Responsible for full project implementation including design, layout, and management of production activities.
- Created marketing campaign that lead to a significant increase in overall sales.
- Acted as liaison between management and clients
- Produced a consistent increase in sales every year
- Surpassed quota in each year (200k, 350k, 500k, 750k)

Sales Manager:
- Responsible for all sales activities including development of new accounts and maintaining existing clients
- Successfully managed a team of three account executives
- Developed and implemented sales strategy, goals, and marketing campaigns
- Established relationships with key executives at customer accounts and vendors
- Surpassed quota in each year (500k, 500k, 500k)
- Sales/Year (650k, 730k, 800k)
- Attended numerous industry conferences and conventions

Sales Director and CEO:
- Met quota (1.5m) despite cutbacks in sales staff
- Responsible for all sales, financial, and operating activities of the organization
- Created management team to empower certain employees and delegate responsibilities
- Assisted with the development of the business plan
- Created an Information Technology initiative to reduce overhead and administrative costs, while increasing production and accounting efficiencies

Education:
BA in History, University of Minnesota, 1993

Activities:
Junior League of Minneapolis (1998-present) - Philanthropic organization
- Co-chaired Winter Soiree 2000
Alpha Phi

AFTER

ELISE HANSON

4982 Madison St., Minneapolis, MN 55401 612-698-2840

OBJECTIVE   To continue a successful sales career for a pharmaceutical or medical equipment manufacturer.

1994–2001   **Rampage Graphics Corp.** [$2M graphics company serving print and advertising industries]
            Sales Manager   1998–2001
            Sales Representative   1994–1998 [Illinois, Iowa, Missouri, and Michigan markets]

Overview...............   After 6 months of sales training at the headquarters plant, I was assigned to Minneapolis and given a group of 35 accounts that had generated under $25,000 the previous 2 years.

BUILDING AN ACCOUNT BASE

 Challenge   My first accounts were poor performers. Over 50% had never purchased services before, and the rest considered us a last resort. My task was to reestablish contact, win favor, and generate orders.

Actions   Relations   • Built meaningful relationships and truly learned customer needs
        Technology   • Created a database and profiled clients
        Pricing   • Built a quote pipeline that grew from 50 to 400 quotes per month

Results   1. Grew revenues 700% to $175,000 per month
        2. Turned 22 accounts into RCG's top 25 revenue generators
        3. Originated 50+ new accounts worth $250K in aggregate sales over 6 years

EXECUTED A PUSH/PULL SELLING STRATEGY TO IMPROVE PROFITABILITY

 Challenge   Our customers thought RGC was a premium-priced service to be used rarely. Additionally, their clients, the end users who generate orders, were price sensitive and resisted quotes on higher margin services.

Response   Overcame purchasing reluctance by:
        • Revealing the value of our services relative to the project need and then proving that this value justified the premium price to meet the client's goals.
        • Starting a teaching sales strategy in which I taught our clients the benefits of our service well enough to convince their customers and pull through a sale.

Results   1. Successfully moved half of all RGC orders from lower margin services to higher profit service sets, essentially doubling our profit margins.
        2. Interest grew so high I created a 2.5-day *Applications Seminar* with 50 paid attendees representing 35 companies. This made us a "best in class" company.

WIN-BACK OF TWO VULNERABLE ACCOUNTS

 Need   Two key clients, representing $100K in annual sales, reduced purchases by 90%.

Response   Met with the president of each company to discover their impression was that RCG was not valuing them as a significant customer. I then implemented a "gold-glove" relationship plan and made them high-priority accounts.

Result   One of the two became a top-10 account and together increased their orders 400%.

As Manager   • Handled full project implementation, i.e., design, layout, and managing production activities
        • Managed a team of 3 account executives
        • Established relations with key executives at customer accounts and vendors
        • Created management team and assisted with developing the business plan

Result   1. As a selling sales manager, surpassed quota in each year from $500K–$800K

Elise Hanson

1993–1994
Overview...............

Admissions Representative, Sᴛ. Pᴀᴜʟ Tᴇᴄʜɴɪᴄᴀʟ Iɴꜱᴛɪᴛᴜᴛᴇ, St. Paul, MN
Market this technical institute to high school students at their schools and in their homes during visits with potential student's parents. Present advantages of attending institute. Used prospecting, sales, follow-up, and closing techniques in securing enrollment.

VOLUNTEER

1997–present

Junior League of Minneapolis—a philanthropy

Event
Cochair Winter *Soiree 2000*

Actions

Result

$34,000 budget   750 attendees
This is the Jr League's largest fund-raising event.
Cold-called corporations for financial donations.
Solicited businesses to supply food, beverages, entertainment, and silent auction prizes.
Generated a total of $50,000 in funds distributed to over 20 charity-based projects.

EDUCATION

BA, History University of Minnesota 1993

Internship   News Reporter

Star Tribune, Minneapolis, MN

References available on request.

ELISE HANSON'S STORY

Success Snapshot:	Elise's only work history was selling foil stamp printing services. Her resume helped her bridge into pharmaceutical sales.
Career Sweet Spot:	Elise now works for one of the largest pharmaceutical companies in the world. She was selected by Merck & Co. from 1,200 candidates.
Trouble Spot Fixed:	She had no medical experience or medical education, yet was able to break into the pharmaceutical industry.
To Use This Chart:	1. Score your resume.
	2. Find Before and After RQI scores in the PYV, MCG, and CPS categories similar to your scores.
	3. Strengthen your weaknesses using our tactics.

BEFORE SCORE				**of 100%**	**Score**
Category I	Prove Your Value	PYV	=	44%	25 of 75
Category II	Met Corporate Goals	MCG	=	33%	10 of 30
Category III	Career Progress Status	CPS	=	67%	20 of 30
	Their RQI Score:			**41%**	**55 of 135**

AFTER SCORE				**of 100%**	**Score**
Category I	Prove Your Value	PYV	=	100%	75 of 75
Category II	Met Corporate Goals	MCG	=	100%	30 of 30
Category III	Career Progress Status	CPS	=	100%	30 of 30
	Our RQI Score:			**100%**	**135 of 135**

CAREER STATS

Career Field:	Sales
Old Title:	Sales Rep
New Title:	Sales Manager
Bridge or Ladder:	Bridge

IMPROVEMENT

From:	Power Puff
To:	Power Pro

KEY

Power Pro:	95% RQI	Power Pansy:	60–80% RQI
Power Prospect:	80–95% RQI	Power Puff:	Below 60% RQI

JENNIFER JOHNSON

Small Corp to Fortune 500

CAREER HIGHLIGHTS

- Salary increase with her new resume: $25,000

- Promoted from account executive to business development manager

- Job search length: four weeks

BEFORE

RQI: 50

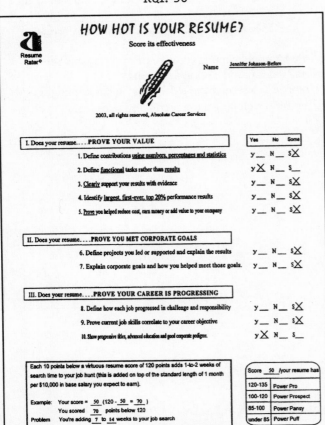

AFTER

RQI: 135

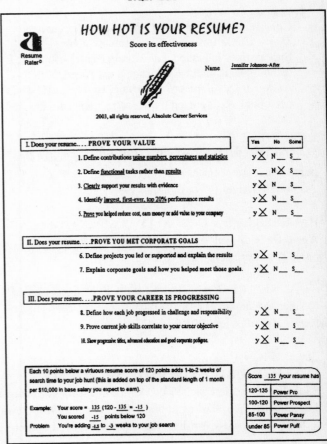

JENNIFER JOHNSON
1289 Sanfernando Dr.
Towanda, CA 47980 314-698-6594

QUALIFICATIONS PROFILE
- Accomplished Sales Professional with a proven record of performance and leadership in the software industry. Creator of innovative solutions.
- Highly effective in presentations to key decision makers.
- Experienced in building relationships/networks with major accounts and business partners.
- Skilled account manager with demonstrated success in creating new business. Dedicated and enthusiastic; committed to exceeding company goals.

EXPERTISE

Software Industry	Innovative Solutions	Customer Relationships & Networks
New Business Development	Account Management	Presentations to Decision Makers

CAREER HIGHLIGHTS
- Promoted to Senior Account Representative at MQSoftware based on exceptional initiative in creating business for a monitoring tool targeting the messaging middleware market. Effectively networked with IBM Sales Representatives and business partners; immediately leveraged company in the marketplace, with projected revenue of *$8.5* million in 1999.
- Established and developed solid relationships with large national and international accounts including *Kansas City Southern Railroad, AIM Funds, US Department of Defense, Sanwa Bank, Hong Kong Bank, Monsanto* and many others.
- Actively prospected and developed new business through presentations to Chief Technical Officers and MIS Directors generating sales of monitoring tool, training and consulting for IBM's MQSeries.
- Delivered effective product presentations that consistently resulted in high closing rate and customer confidence. Gained strong knowledge of mainframe and distributed network systems; created innovative solutions tailored to each customer's network.
- Consistently earned *3,000 Club Award* for outstanding sales performance over two-plus-years. Named to *President's Honor Circle* for exceeding company goals.
- Successfully launched a new branch sales office for Bankers Life by implementing creative prospecting and selling techniques. Branch sales office grew from 207th to 12th in overall sales production in first year.
- As Agent Development Associate, Bankers Life & Casualty Company, designed and led all new agent training for 70 personnel. Recognized by Vice President of Sales and Marketing for developing a top producing sales team.

EXPERIENCE
MQSOFTWARE INCORPORATED, Minneapolis, MN
Senior Account Manager 1998 to Present
Account Manager (three months) 1998

BANKERS LIFE & CASUALTY COMPANY, Edina, MN
Agent Development Associate 1997 to 1998
Sales Representative 1995 to 1997

ST. ANNE'S RESIDENTIAL SERVICE, Minneapolis, MN
Resident Manager 1993 to 1995
Resident Counselor 1991 to 1993

EDUCATION
ST. CLOUD STATE UNIVERSITY, St. Cloud, MN
Bachelor of Arts in Psychology; Minor in Business Management
TRADE SHOWS: Participant in IBM Messaging Middleware Conferences 1998 to Present
COMPUTER: MS Word • Excel • PowerPoint • Internet • E-mail

JENNIFER JOHNSON
1289 Sanfernando Dr. Towanda, IL 47980   847-698-6594

OBJECTIVE   To continue selling and applying planning and execution strengths to account development activities.

STRENGTHS
- Systems Knowledge
- Software Sales
- Executive Presentations
- Relationship Management
- Competitive Trending
- Account Penetration
- Solution Selling
- Consulting Sales

SELLING EXPERIENCE

11/99 - 10/01
Overview..............

SALES EXECUTIVE   **TUSC** – an Oracle Certified Solution Partner
Sold remote Database Administration (DBA) software, management consulting services and technical support to corporate CTOs, CIOs and Directors of IT. Average sell netted a $40,000 contract with potential to double the account value by selling add-on consulting services, trainings and mentoring program elements.

| Challenge 1 | | Influencing IT Executives & Database Managers that TUSC's RemoteDBA program didn't outsource their function or that the service did not replace their role. |
| Response | | Won trust and diplomatically proved before each sale that our relationship had significant strategic value to their ongoing business operations. |

Challenge 2 — As the first RemoteDBA sales executive, I created the initial marketing strategy (via trade shows, cold calling and email campaigns) to market TUSC to the industry. Due to my success, a year later 3 new sales reps were hired whom I trained and mentored.
Response — Prospecting efforts increased contacts from -0- to 4,000+ qualified leads in a year.

Challenge 3 — Building Partnerships — Networked with top technology contacts to uncover referrals and identify which companies were seeking strategic partners.
Response — Compaq — Commitment to use TUSC on Oracle pursuits. **Result**: FY02 sales will be $10MM.

Response — SalesLogix — Developed relationship and nurtured it to where TUSC supports their 3,200 Oracle database customers. **Result:** This first strategic partnership is now the model for all joint-relationships.

Result
- Sales — Initiated 32 contracts worth a total of $1.2MM.
- Renewels — 92% of the clients renewed their contracts.
- Clients Won — • WorldCom • The Boeing Co. • Acxiom Corp. • Fed Reserve • Williams Energy • PayPal

6/98 - 11/99
Overview..............

SENIOR ACCOUNT MANAGER   **MQSOFTWARE INC.**, Minneapolis, MN
an IBM premier business partner
I sold QPasa! which monitors IBM's messaging middleware product - MQSeries. My role was to consult with CTOs, CIOs and MIS Directors to learn their mainframe and distributed network systems and leverage MQSoftware in the marketplace. Attended IBM Messaging Middleware Conferences (1998-2000)

Result — Average sale: $60,000   Clients Won –
- AIM Funds
- US DOD
- Sanwa Bank
- Monsanto
- K.C. Southern RR
- Hong Kong Bank

1995 - 1997
Overview..............

SALES REPRESENTATIVE/TRAINER   **BANKERS LIFE & CASUALTY CO.**, Edina, MN
Designed prospecting and selling techniques to open a branch sales office and train 70 sales staff.

Result — Branch sales office grew from 207th to 12th in sales production in first year.
Personally generated $1,600,000 in annually premiums.
Member of *the 3,000 Club*. President's *Honor Circle*.

1991 - 1993   **RESIDENT MANAGER & COUNSELOR**   ST. ANNE'S RESIDENTIAL SERVICE, Minneapolis, MN

EDUCATION   1991   B.A., Psychology; Minor, Business Management, St. Cloud State University, St. Cloud, MN

JENNIFER JOHNSON'S STORY

Success Snapshot: Jennifer sold technology consulting services for a small company and wanted to work for a Fortune 500 corporation. Her new resume led to a job with GE.

Career Sweet Spot: Jennifer is now a business development specialist in GE's Information Technology Solutions Group.

Trouble Spot Fixed: Overcame the negative stigma of small company experience to appeal to a multinational corporation.

To Use This Chart:
1. Score your resume.
2. Find Before and After RQI scores in the PYV, MCG, and CPS categories similar to your scores.
3. Strengthen your weaknesses using our tactics.

BEFORE SCORE			of 100%	Score
Category I	Prove Your Value	PYV = 15%		20 of 75
Category II	Met Corporate Goals	MCG = 33%		10 of 30
Category III	Career Progress Status	CPS = 67%		20 of 30
	Their RQI Score:		37%	**50 of 135**

AFTER SCORE			of 100%	Score
Category I	Prove Your Value	PYV = 100%		75 of 75
Category II	Met Corporate Goals	MCG = 100%		30 of 30
Category III	Career Progress Status	CPS = 100%		30 of 30
	Our RQI Score:		100%	**135 of 135**

CAREER STATS

Career Field:	Sales
Old Title:	Account Executive
New Title:	BDM
Bridge or Ladder:	Ladder

IMPROVEMENT

From:	Power Puff
To:	Power Pro

KEY

Power Pro:	95% RQI	Power Pansy:	60–80% RQI
Power Prospect:	80–95% RQI	Power Puff:	Below 60% RQI

APRIL LAWRENCE

From Hertz Rent-a-Car to Director of Human Resources

CAREER HIGHLIGHTS

- Salary increase with her new resume: $27,000

- Promoted to director HR

- Job search length: six weeks

BEFORE
RQI: 15

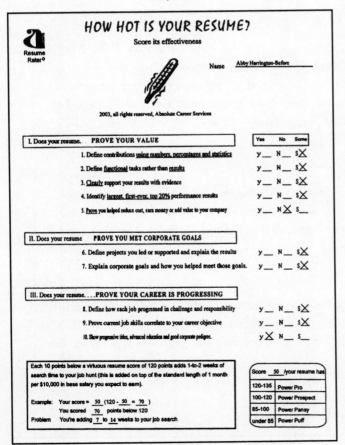

AFTER
RQI: 85

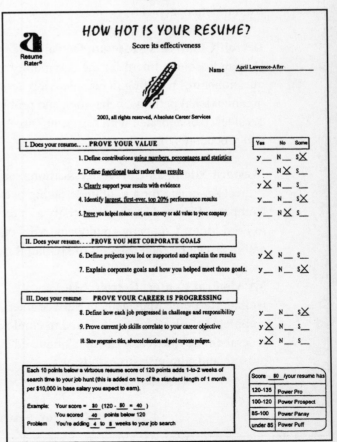

APRIL LAWRENCE
1479 East Bay Dr.
Detroit, MI 48226
313-778-5629

EDUCATION

Western Michigan University, Kalamazoo, MI.

Bachelor of Science degree in Business Management/Human Resources awarded in May 1994. Courses include Organizational Behavior, Personnel Planning and Selection, Labor Relations and Law, and Compensation Administration.

Vice President of Programming for the Student Chapter of Society for Human Resource Management. Organized eight professional speaker engagements and arranged group participation in community events and fundraising activities.

WORK EXPERIENCE

Hertz Rent-A-Car, Detroit, MI   **May 1994–July 1999**

Management Trainee in a nine person branch office. Managed daily branch office operations, handled front-line customer service, employee scheduling and training, inside/outside sales and marketing, and accounts receivables. Pursued and secured numerous outside sales accounts gaining recognition from top management.

Detroit Children's Museum, Detroit, MI   **January 1994–May 1994**

Human Resource Intern for the community museum. Created and administered job analysis questionnaires resulting in complete job descriptions for all staff members. Analyzed the museum's organizational patterns, behaviors, and problems and presented recommendations to the Board of Trustees. Collaborated with Assistant Director and participating interns to reconstruct the policies and procedures manual.

Western Michigan University, Kalamazoo, MI   **March 1994**

Project Associate for a joint undertaking between Western Michigan University and Ford Motor Company. Selected by the University as a team member to administer employee satisfaction surveys to Ford Motor Company employees. All work was completed at the Indianapolis manufacturing plant and overseen by their director of Human Resources.

VA Medical Center, Detroit, MI   **May 1993–August 1993**

Human Resource Management Service Intern for the medical center. Updated current job descriptions, completed a salary survey, assisted in employee orientation, and was introduced to OWCP, EEO, and federal employment law issues. Conducted quality assurance reviews and prepared reports for the nursing and administrative divisions.

References Available on Request

April L. Lawrence

1479 East Bay Dr., Detroit, MI 48226   (313) 778-5629

OBJECTIVE

A career opportunity in the field of human resources; a position capitalizing on operational management, client support, and staff development skills.

SUMMARY

Management experience, academic qualifications, and a history of building successful business networks and a focus on problem-solving capabilities. Career emphasis is to develop and maintain human resource services that surpass corporate objectives.

EDUCATION
5/94

B.S., <u>Business Management/Human Resources</u>, Western Michigan University, Kalamazoo, MI
Coursework: • Organizational Behavior   • Personnel Planning and Selection
                • Labor Relations and Law   • Compensation Administration

V.P. of Programming—Student Chapter, <u>Society for Human Resource Management</u>
Organized professional speaking engagements on: • Professional Development
• Internships   • Candidate Selection   • Career Stress

EXPERIENCE
5/94–7/95

Management Trainee, HERTZ RENT-A-CAR, Detroit, MI
Managed daily branch operations, handled frontline customer service, employee training, inside/outside sales, marketing, and account receivables in a 9-person office.

PROJECT   Pursued outside sales accounts with all Schaumburg area hotels.
RESULTS   Secured exclusive arrangements with 8 hotels and gained recognition from
                district and regional managers.

PROJECT   Reorganized satellite branch operations.
RESULTS   Redesigned the document routing and revenue tracking systems to streamline
                operations and eliminate errors.

INTERNSHIPS
1/94–5/94

Human Resource Intern, DETROIT CHILDREN'S MUSEUM, Detroit, MI
PROJECT   Created and administered job questionnaires for all staff. Analyzed
                museum's organization, communications, and staffing problems.
RESULTS   Wrote new job descriptions and implemented changes in work conditions,
                staff communications, and performance appraisals. Collaborated with the
                assistant director to rewrite the policies and procedures manual.

3/94

Associate, WESTERN MICHIGAN UNIVERSITY, Kalamazoo, MI
PROJECT   Selected as a team member in a joint effort between **Western U. and Ford
                Motor Co.** to administer employee satisfaction surveys to 20% of their
                UAW employees.

5/93–8/93

Human Resource Management Intern, VA MEDICAL CENTER, Detroit, MI
Updated job descriptions, completed a salary survey, and assisted employee orientation.
Introduced to OWCP, EEO, and federal employment law compliance issues.

PROJECT   Developed and conducted two QA records reviews.
RESULTS   Wrote reports regarding findings of review for the Department of Human
                Resources and the Department of Nursing Administration.

APRIL LAWRENCE'S STORY

Success Snapshot: April, a recent college grad, had a degree in human resources, yet worked as a manager trainee for Hertz Rent-A-Car, a job completely outside of her field of interest. Her new resume demonstrated that her education and internships could support a career change into human resources.

Career Sweet Spot: Six weeks after sending her resume out, she was hired as the HR director of United Healthcare.

Trouble Spot Fixed: Bridging from the car rental business into her ideal career path of human resources.

To Use This Chart:
1. Score your resume.
2. Find Before and After RQI scores in the PYV, MCG, and CPS categories similar to your scores.
3. Strengthen your weaknesses using our tactics.

BEFORE SCORE			of 100%	Score
Category I	Prove Your Value	PYV = 0%		0 of 75
Category II	Met Corporate Goals	MCG = 33%		10 of 30
Category III	Career Progress Status	CPS = 17%		5 of 30
	Their RQI Score:		**11%**	**15 of 135**

AFTER SCORE			of 100%	Score
Category I	Prove Your Value	PYV = 53%		40 of 75
Category II	Met Corporate Goals	MCG = 67%		20 of 30
Category III	Career Progress Status	CPS = 83%		25 of 30
	Our RQI Score:		**63%**	**85 of 135**

CAREER STATS

Career Field:	Human Resources
Old Title:	Manager Trainee
New Title:	Director HR
Bridge or Ladder:	Ladder and Bridge

IMPROVEMENT

From:	Power Puff
To:	Power Prospect

KEY

Power Pro:	95% RQI	Power Pansy:	60–80% RQI
Power Prospect:	80–95% RQI	Power Puff:	Below 60% RQI

CAROLINE REAGAN

Bridge from a Dying Industry to a New Industry

CAREER HIGHLIGHTS

- Salary increase with her new resume: $15,000

- Was able to leave a shrinking industry

- She said her career was revitalized

BEFORE
RQI: 20

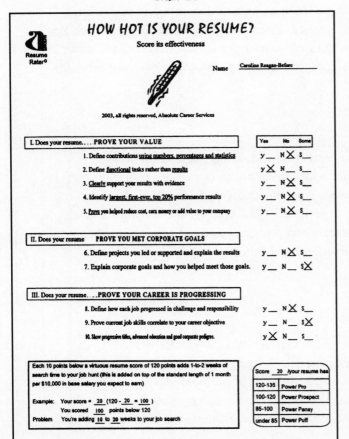

AFTER
RQI: 135

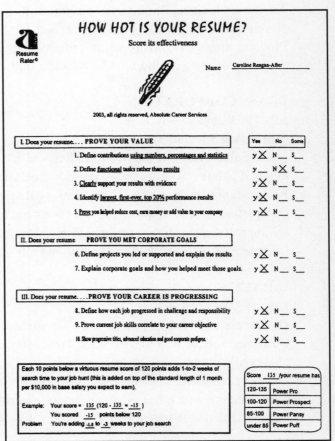

CAROLINE REAGAN
2562 Treetop Lane
Madison, WI 53515
608-558-4970

JOB OBJECTIVE

A responsible and challenging career opportunity, which utilizes my educational background, experience, and will provide potential for future advancement and professional growth with a strong Preference for people contact.

EXPERIENCE

DIAMOND PET FOOD

October 1997 to January 1999

Sales Representative—Pet Food Products

Territory—Illinois, and Indiana. Sold and represented five lines of pet food. Responsibilities included opening new accounts' and maintaining existing accounts. Sales support and customer service included an aggressive demo program implemented, employee-store training programs and value added promotions for the retailer and consumer.

NATURAL CARE PET PRODUCTS

June 1996 to October 1997

Sales Representative—Pet Food Products

Territory—Indiana, Illinois and Wisconsin. Responsible for opening new accounts and maintaining current accounts through sales support and customer service. Distributor support for Natural Care Pet Products through demo programs, promotions, pet shows and sales representation. Heavy customer support providing a solid foundation and a high confidence level with pet stores to back our products.

BRASS CORPORATION

July 1993–June 1996

Marketing Specialist

Inside Sales/Customer Service Rep. Responsible for marketing and selling, brass strip through inbound phone resources and to provide the customer with conscientious customer service. Responding to daily customer inquiries, order processing, problem solving and trouble shooting. Completion of orders, tracers, return forms and use of an IBM3 178C computer. Utilizing suggestive selling techniques, diplomacy, and to maintain a constant and positive customer service image. Intermediary between customer needs and mill production capabilities.

U-HAUL

May 1992–April 1993

Corporate and Origin Relocation Coordinator

Customer Service Rep./Inside Sales. Putting together moves from start to finish. Experienced in all phases of moving—origin, destination, and corporate accounts. Large range of duties, including phone survey's, estimates, extremely heavy people/phone contact with lots of problem solving and inside sales. Dealing with other agents, shippers, and national account representatives. Very fast paced and detail oriented with lots of public relations. Full knowledge of local, intrastate, and interstate moves.

Caroline Reagan

TAU KAPPA EPSILON FRATERNITY
July 1991–April 1992
Assistant to the Vice President
Various projects relating to the Fraternity. Heavy organizational skills, light supervision.

PRINT GRAPHICS, INC.
January 1990–January 1991
Sales and Account Representative
Building of clients through cold calls and appointments. Responsibility of helping and satisfying clients printing needs and working with them to ensure repeat business and additional orders.

CENTURY 21
June 1988–January 1990
Administrative Assistant
Real Estate advertising for Homes <u>Magazine</u> and <u>Star-News</u> newspaper. All processing and closing of listings. Heavy paperwork, people contact and problem solving.

CHEESCAKE FACTORY
September 1987–January 1990
Waitress and Bartender
Heavy people contact, organization and problem solving.

CHICAGO BOARD OF REALTORS
January 1986–July 1987
Administrative Assistant
Large range of duties relating to Board business. Took care of membership, RPAC, and the design and printing of The Board of Realtor's Newsletter. Responsible for organizing and setting up numerous Board social and business functions. Heavy problem solving and strong membership relations.

ILLINI SPORTING GOODS
August 1981–August 1984 and again October 1985–May 1987
Salesperson/Merchandiser
Heavy people contact. Inventory, restocking, straightening and demonstration of merchandise. Creating displays and designing store windows.

<u>EDUCATION</u>
University of Wisconsin–Madison, WI
Major: Business/Advertising 1984–1985

CAROLINE T. REAGAN

2562 Treetop Lane, Madison, WI 53515   608-558-4970

OBJECTIVE

Sales, Business Development, & Marketing

1/99–present   *Territory Sales Manager*   **PRECISE PET PRODUCTS**

Sell $1.2 million annually to a base of 125 accounts across Illinois, Wisconsin, and Indiana.

Challenge ❶   Took over a struggling territory that had experienced a 20% revenue decline over the past 2 years.

Solution	Executed a series of sales and marketing programs to convert our customers from the competition. Strategies included supporting retailers as follows:	
Training	• Demo Program	Recruited and hired 25 demonstrators
Sampling	• Free Product Offer	Convinced management to invest in samples
	Frequent Feeder Cards	Used to build consumer habit
Marketing	• Marketing Collateral	Created Top-10 lists
	Print campaign	Ads, coupons, and brochures

Results
- Increased revenues by $200,000 (17% increase).
- 50 accounts have made Precise Pet their focus product.
- Competitors copied my sample program and began to use Top-10 lists.

Challenge ❷   Introduced two key price increases. One was 75% (cat food), and the other was 25% (dog food).

Solution   Presented cat food with money-back guarantee and dog food increases using coupons to soften initial consumer reaction and protect the retailer.

Results   Achieved 100% sell-in (only 1 cat food client loss) and gained 60 new cat accounts.

10/97–1/99   *Sales Representative*   **DIAMOND PET FOOD**

Sold 5 product lines in Illinois and Indiana. Executed business development strategies, a demo program, store employee training, and value-added promotions delivered to retailers and consumers.

Challenge ❸   Diamond Pet Food lost their largest client, PetCare, who was acquired by Petco and choose not to carry our product line, Sensible Choice, until a corporate agreement was signed a year later.

Solution   Petco managers lack authority to give shelf space for promotions, so revenue building came from recruiting, training, and managing 50 product demonstrators.

Results   Increased sales 15% relative to year-to-date numbers.

Challenge ❹   Developing a secondary product line, Excel.

Solution   Cold-called accounts, conducted personal demos, and initiated marketing actions such as the first-ever Top-5 list with coupon attached and free 5-lb bag trials.

Results   Doubled sales within 5 months and opened 25 new accounts.

Caroline T. Reagan

6/96–10/97   *Sales Representative*   **NATURAL CARE PET PRODUCTS**

Territory—Indiana, Illinois, and Wisconsin (in 4 months I was transferred to the 3rd largest territory)
Opened and maintained accounts. Distributor support using demo programs, promotions, pet
shows, and sales representation. Heavy customer support with pet stores to back our products.

Challenge ❺   Distributor changeover.

Solution   Worked with regional sales manager to make a successful distributor change
Result   Over 90% of accounts successfully changed to new distributor

EDUCATION   Pursued a B.S. in Advertising and Business, University of Wisconsin, Madison, WI

CAROLINE REAGAN'S STORY

Success Snapshot: Caroline sold pet food products to a shrinking market and wanted to change fields. She took a job with the global leader in manufacturing pallets and plastic containers, a completely new industry.

Career Sweet Spot: She told us that the money she spent on the resume was the best money she spent last year and received dozens of job opportunities. It also broke her out of a stagnant career path and into a new industry.

Trouble Spot Fixed: Career stagnation and uncompleted college degree.

To Use This Chart:
1. Score your resume.
2. Find Before and After RQI scores in the PYV, MCG, and CPS categories similar to your scores.
3. Strengthen your weaknesses using our tactics.

BEFORE SCORE			of 100%	Score
Category I	Prove Your Value	PYV =	0%	0 of 75
Category II	Met Corporate Goals	MCG =	17%	5 of 30
Category III	Career Progress Status	CPS =	50%	15 of 30
	Their RQI Score:		**15%**	**20 of 135**

AFTER SCORE			of 100%	Score
Category I	Prove Your Value	PYV =	100%	75 of 75
Category II	Met Corporate Goals	MCG =	100%	30 of 30
Category III	Career Progress Status	CPS =	100%	30 of 30
	Our RQI Score:		**100%**	**135 of 135**

CAREER STATS

Career Field:	Sales
Old Title:	Sales Rep
New Title:	Territory Manager
Bridge or Ladder:	Bridge

IMPROVEMENT

From:	Power Puff
To:	Power Pro

KEY

Power Pro:	95% RQI	Power Pansy:	60–80% RQI
Power Prospect:	80–95% RQI	Power Puff:	Below 60% RQI

SCOTT WASHBURN

From Non-Profit into Government Job in Purchasing

CAREER HIGHLIGHTS

- Salary increase with his new resume: $12,000

- Promoted from a nonprofit association to goverment negotiator

- Job search length: three months

BEFORE

RQI: 25

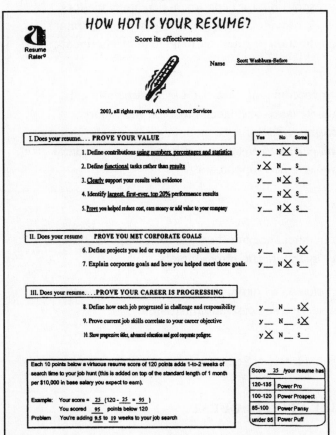

AFTER

RQI: 135

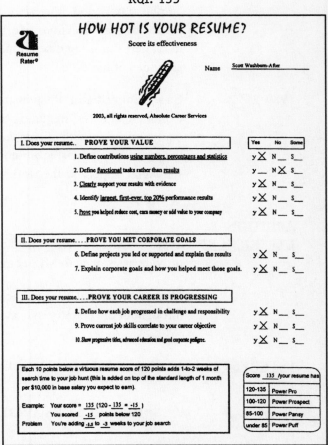

SCOTT WASHBURN
2550 Plainfeild Rd
Minneapolis, MN 55401
612-339-0284

EDUCATION: University St. Thomas Minnesota State College
Bachelor of Arts Degree: Associate of Arts Degree:
May, 1989 May, 1987

WORK EXPERIENCE:

1994–present **National Arbitration Forum Minneapolis. MN:**
Assistant Regional Vice President. Provide supervision of all case work, giving advice and assistance to administrators; participation in hiring and promotion decisions; provide appropriate training for employees and arbitrators; involved in all matters related to personnel; assist in the recruitment of qualified arbitrators; Participation in educational, membership, promotional and marketing activities of the office.

1992–1994 Commercial Department Supervisor. Supervision of departmental case administration and other activities; responsible for department personnel matters; review of draft decisions of arbitrators; provide advice and assistance to arbitrators in matters requiring discretionary application of rules; participate in promotional activities of the office.

1989–1992 Case Administrator. Responsible for coordinating caseload of Construction and Commercial cases, including the maintenance of financial records and reports; communication with clients, arbitrators, and attorneys; attending hearings to observe the process and assist arbitrators and parties to ensure compliance with procedural standards; supervise the work of any assigned support staff.

ADDITIONAL EXPERIENCE: Systems Operator. Responsible for maintenance of office AS/400 computer system; provide assistance to MIS computer operators and programmers.

Member National Training Team. Selected by national headquarters to train offices throughout the country in customer service and case administration.

INTERESTS: Member and officer—Merry Gangsters Literary Society.

REFERENCES AVAILABLE UPON REQUEST

SCOTT J. WASHBURN

2550 Plainfield Rd., Minneapolis, MN 55401 612-379-0684

OBJECTIVE To continue a management career for a company that will allow me to correlate legal understanding with public relations, business management, and strategic planning skills.

SUMMARY Expert administration, staff development, service integration, and organization skills allow me to achieve strategic objectives, resolve complex issues, and defend organizational position. Use analytical and leadership abilities to achieve strong results and network with both management and clients to determine effective solutions to problems.

EXPERIENCE
1989–1998

NATIONAL ARBITRATION FORUM, Minneapolis, MN
94–98 *Asst. Regional V.P.* • 92–94 *Commercial Supervisor* • 89–92 *Case Administrator*
Managed arbitration caseflow for 600 cases annually. Selected arbitrators from a pool of 2,500 candidates and assigned case administrators. Led educational, membership, and marketing activities that increased billings 25%. Counseled parties on the process of mediating construction, commercial, real estate, and securities contract disputes. Reviewed contracts to determine complexity and urgency. Provided expert testimony at hearings as needed.

Admin	Quality initiatives attained a 98.5% success rate of completing cases on time and within rule format, applicable laws, and appropriate contract provisions.
Systems	Assisted MIS programmers in upgrading, troubleshooting and maintaining the AS-400 mainframe system.
Training	Train arbitrators on conducting hearings under appropriate rules. Train staff on accurate and time-delineated case administration.
Personnel	Built H.R. staff of 15 by matching personnel skills with functional needs. Personnel actions included hiring, promoting, training, applicant screening, assessment, and conflict resolution.

PROJECT *1* NATIONAL TRAINING PROGRAM—Selected by the National Advisory Committee to present customer service techniques and train Detroit, L.A., Philadelphia, and Boston office staff.

PROJECT *2* MARKETING CAMPAIGN—Created the Minnesota Real Estate Buyer/Seller Mediation program for Northwest's association of 3,500 realtors.

PROJECT *3* CREATING STATE BRANCHES—Created 2 regional processing centers (RPCs). South Central RPC grew volume from 200 cases to 2,000 per year for 5 states and the South Eastern RPC grew from 125 cases to 800 per year for a 6-state region.

Case Administrator   1989–1992
Coordinated cases impacting Construction and Commercial disputes, maintained financial records and reports; communicated with clients, arbitrators and attorneys; attended hearings to assist arbitrators and to ensure compliance with procedural standards.

PUBLIC SPEAKING Minneapolis Bar Association, Construction Law Committee Meeting
Minneapolis Bar Association, Continuing Legal Education

PERSONAL Member and Officer, Merry Gangsters Literary Society.
• Featured guest, The Learning Channel *Rouge's Gallery* special on Al Capone, 1996
• Published article: "Al Capone and Friends," IASOC's Criminal Organization, 1995
• Featured guest, Art & Entertainment, The Al Capone Biography, 1995

EDUCATION B.A.,   Criminal Justice, University of St. Thomas   1989

SCOTT WASHBURN'S STORY

Success Snapshot: Scott had one job for nine years, in the field of dispute resolution at the National Arbitration Forum. He was vulnerable to career stagnation and job lock.

Career Sweet Spot: Within six months after we rewrote Scott's resume, the City of Minneapolis, Department of Purchases hired him as a contract negotiator.

Trouble Spot Fixed: Overcoming narrow career experience and winning a high-level government job.

To Use This Chart:
1. Score your resume.
2. Find Before and After RQI scores in the PYV, MCG, and CPS categories similar to your scores.
3. Strengthen your weaknesses using our tactics.

BEFORE SCORE		of 100%	Score
Category I	Prove Your Value	PYV = 0%	0 of 75
Category II	Met Corporate Goals	MCG = 17%	5 of 30
Category III	Career Progress Status	CPS = 67%	20 of 30
	Their RQI Score:	**19%**	**25 of 135**

AFTER SCORE		of 100%	Score
Category I	Prove Your Value	PYV = 100%	75 of 75
Category II	Met Corporate Goals	MCG = 100%	20 of 30
Category III	Career Progress Status	CPS = 100%	30 of 30
	Our RQI Score:	**100%**	**135 of 135**

CAREER STATS

Career Field:	Municipal Negotiator
Old Title:	Assistant VP
New Title:	Contract Negotiator
Bridge or Ladder:	Bridge

IMPROVEMENT

From:	Power Puff
To:	Power Pro

KEY

Power Pro:	95% RQI	Power Pansy:	60–80% RQI
Power Prospect:	80–95% RQI	Power Puff:	Below 60% RQI

ERIC WERNER

Recent College Grad to a Job at a Top Consulting Firm

CAREER HIGHLIGHTS

• Salary increase with his new resume: $95,000

• Promoted from college student to national account manager

• Job search length: seamless from graduation

BEFORE

RQI: 50

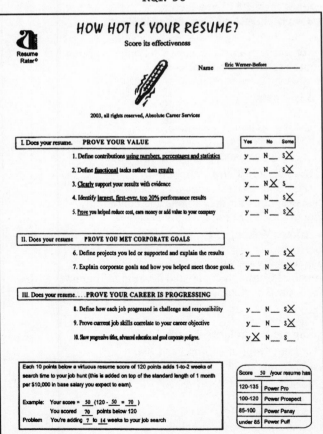

AFTER

RQI: 135

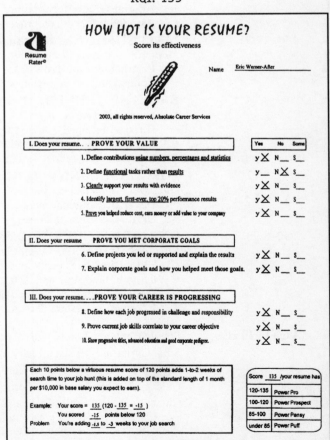

Eric Werner
5333 Redwing Ct. LakeGeorge, IL
609-238-7524

EDUCATION 1996–Present	**Depaul University; Chicago, Illinois** Master of Science, Health Systems Management Expected date of graduation—August, 1998 Graduate Certificate in Healthcare Ethics—June, 1998
1987–1993	**University of Wisconsin**; **Milwaukee, Wisconsin** Bachelor of Science, History and History of Science
EXPERIENCE 9/97–2/98	**SINAI HOSPITAL; Chicago, Illinois** *Administrative Project Assistant-Internship, Women's and Children's Hospital* • Assisted administrative manager with operational responsibilities • Collected data and performed monthly fiscal reports involving the clinical units • Conducted mandatory staff in-service training sessions in preparation for JCAHO • Developed database for redesign initiative of Labor and Delivery services
6/97–9/97	*Administrative Project Internship, Sinai Children's Heart Center* • Updated, enhanced, and maintained the Sinai Internet Home Page • Aided in the development and marketing of educational material for the Internet • Developed queries and reports for the cardiology database
9/96–6/97	*Project Assistant Internship, Information Services* • Involved in the development of the patient confidentiality handbook for Sinai Hospital • Provided support in process reengineering
12/95–9/96	**ST. FRANCIS HOSPITAL; Milwaukee, Wisconsin** *Assistant to Manager Risk Management Department* • Administered safety and fire inspections for the 517-bed facility • Assisted in the development of the Bomb Threat and Tornado Risk Plans
4/94–12/95	**IAMS COMPANY; Dayton, Ohio** *Manager trainee, .Management Development Program-Continental Baking Company* • Restructured sales routes for the Southwestern Wisconsin region • Trained and developed new sales representatives
7/93–4/94	**BAGELS FOREVER; Madison, Wisconsin** *Executive Vice President* • Hired and trained 7 salaried managers and 50 hourly personnel • Increased revenues from $1M to $1.5M per year • Created and instituted organization's employee handbook and benefit plan
8/91–8/92	**WISCONSIN UNION DIRECTORATE; Madison, Wisconsin** *Director of Science and Society Committee/Food Service Committee Chairman* • Developed and marketed educational programs for the campus and community • Drafted recommendations pertaining to the $11 M Food Service Budget
2/90–8/90	**GE MEDICAL SYSTEMS; Milwaukee, Wisconsin** *Customer Programs Associate/Sales Assistant* • Closed 50+ sales leads for GE's teleradiology system • Cross trained staff with Interdepartmental Communication and Learning Programs • Designed and implemented the GE Medical Systems Human Resources Computer Information System Directory
ACTIVITIES	People Centered Teams Workshop: Healing the Workplace—March 1998 Sinai Geriatric Interdisciplinary Team Training Program—Summer 1998 American College of Health Care Executives, member Chicago Health Executives Forum, member Chicago Clinical Ethics Programs, member
SKILLS	Word processing, database management, and spreadsheet-proficient

ERIC W. WERNER

5333 Redwing Ct., Lake George, IL 60531 ☎ 609-238-7524

OBJECTIVE   To capitalize on proven abilities to exceed revenue goals, streamline operations, and market complex products and services within a team-based environment.

EXPERIENCE
8/96–PRESENT

Student Consultant   SINAI HOSPITAL, Chicago, IL
PROJECTS   I participated in the following 5 strategic and operational projects for the Sinai System for Health, which consists of hospitals and outpatient services serving 3 million people.

① PROJECT   ***Internet Marketing Multimedia Campaign for Sinai, Children's Heart Center***
Encompassing 19 hospitals and clinics. Tasked by Sinai's department director to team with consultants and develop an education-info marketing strategy that would increase patient population at the Heart Center.
RESULT   Patient load increased 5–10% and web page hits doubled within three months.

② PROJECT   ***Implementing the Agfa-Gavert Image Archiving System***
Part of a team of three consultants who conducted a cost/benefit analysis and wrote a two-prong implementation strategy.
RESULT   Presentation to director of radiology secured approval of our program, which includes a $2,300,000 budget and is currently in the final phase of implementation.

③ PROJECT   ***OB/GYN Revenue Program***
As part of the Sinai 2000 Initiative (encompassing 100+ departments and is projected to reduce operating costs by $200 million in three years), I participated in redesigning the labor and delivery services.
RESULT   Action steps will improve patient flow and customer service, and are projected to increase department revenues by up to $16,400,000 annually.

④ PROJECT   ***Hospital Staff Inservice Training (Women's and Children's Hospital)***
Taught in-service sessions to prepare staff for the annual JCAHO audit.
Topics   □ OSHA Bloodborne Pathogens & TB   □ OSHA Hazard Communications
□ Infection Control and Radiation Safety   □ Patient Rights

⑤ PROJECT   ***Cost Management Initiative***
Submitted a proposal to the purchasing director of Sinai that outlined monetary saving opportunities in the areas of space utilization and energy consumption.
RESULT   When plan is approved it will save between $2,000,000 and $10,000,000 annually.

12/95–9/96   **Assistant to the Risk Manager**, ST. FRANCIS HOSPITAL, Milwaukee, WI
Overview   Educated employees on risk plans for this 517-bed facility.

4/94–12/95   **Executive Management Trainee**, IAMS COMPANY, Dayton, OH
Overview   Managed a staff of 24 route sales reps in a $13,000,000 two-region territory.

PROJECT   ***Sales Route Restructure***
Analyzed 800 stops, identified route inefficiencies as well as new client potential.
RESULT   Increased route stops 5%, earning up to $500K more a year without new staff.

7/93–4/94	**Executive V.P.**	BAGELS FOREVER, Madison, WI
	Overview	Hired and trained 7 salaried managers and 50 hourly personnel for a three-property operation.
	PROJECT	***Sales Agreement with SYSCO Foods*** Initiated contact with the purchasing manager of SYSCO to secure a wholesale purchase agreement.
	RESULT	Unit sales of product increased gross revenues from $1M to $1.5M per year.

2/90–8/90	**Sales Associate**	GE MEDICAL SYSTEMS, Milwaukee, WI
	Overview	Conducted a national product introduction rollout of the teleradiology system for diagnostic imaging and implemented new promotional programs as part of the remarketing task force. **Results:** Closed 50 sales worth $1,250,000 while maintaining a closing ratio of 90%.
	PROJECT	Created the first Human Resources Computer I.S. Directory. Designed this system that was implemented divisionwide throughout GE Medical Systems.
	RESULT	*Won Business Driver of the Quarter Award.*
	PROJECT	Conducted Competitive Market Survey & Direct Marketing Program. Surveyed performance and service issues of 200+ CT Mobile Units.
	RESULT	Qualified 10 sales leads and netted 2 sales generating $3,000,000 in new revenues.

EDUCATION

8/98

M.S., HEALTH SYSTEMS MANAGEMENT   DEPAULUNIVERSITY, Chicago, IL

Program Emphasis: A practitioner-teacher model that integrates theory, practice, and research and is considered the only one of its kind in the United States.

Graduate Thesis: Productivity and Performance Evaluation of People-Centered Teams: A pre/post-study of 285 laboratory staff members of RPSLMC.

1993

B.S., HISTORY OF SCIENCE   UNIVERSITY OF WISCONSIN, Milwaukee, WI

Awards   Received 2 full scholarships for Outstanding Leadership & Scholastic Ability.

MEMBERSHIPS

- American College of Health Care Executives
- Chicago Health Executives Forum
- Chicago Clinical Ethics Programs

TRAINING

Sinai Geriatric Interdisciplinary Team Training Program

References available on request.

ERIC WERNER'S STORY

Success Snapshot: Eric was graduating from DePaul University with a masters in healthcare administration. His eclectic career needed to correspond to his new educational achievements.

Career Sweet Spot: Eric's new resume won him a coveted job, prior to graduation, with PriceWaterhouseCoopers as a national account manager. Starting salary and bonus near six-figures.

Trouble Spot Fixed: Converting college internship into viably attractive work experience.

To Use This Chart:
1. Score your resume.
2. Find Before and After RQI scores in the PYV, MCG, and CPS categories similar to your scores.
3. Strengthen your weaknesses using our tactics.

BEFORE SCORE		**of 100%**	**Score**
Category I	Prove Your Value	PYV = 27%	20 of 75
Category II	Met Corporate Goals	MCG = 100%	10 of 30
Category III	Career Progress Status	CPS = 100%	20 of 30
	Their RQI Score:	**37%**	**50 of 135**

AFTER SCORE		**of 100%**	**Score**
Category I	Prove Your Value	PYV = 100%	75 of 75
Category II	Met Corporate Goals	MCG = 100%	30 of 30
Category III	Career Progress Status	CPS = 100%	30 of 30
	Our RQI Score:	**100%**	**135 of 135**

CAREER STATS

Career Field:	Health Care/IT
Old Title:	Student
New Title:	Nat'l. Acct. Manager
Bridge or Ladder:	Ladder

IMPROVEMENT

From:	Power Puff
To:	Power Pro

KEY

Power Pro:	95% RQI	Power Pansy:	60–80% RQI
Power Prospect:	80–95% RQI	Power Puff:	Below 60% RQI

CHUCK RANDALL

Unemployed Construction Worker to Construction Project Manager

CAREER HIGHLIGHTS

- Salary increase with his new resume: $70,000

- Promoted to project superintendent

- Job search length: eight weeks

BEFORE
RQI: 20

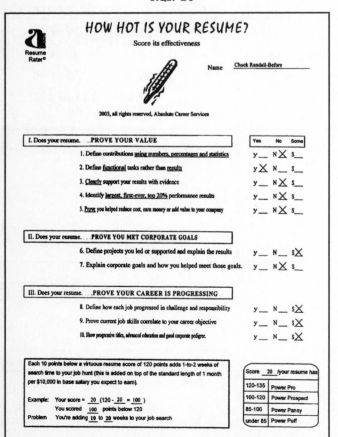

AFTER
RQI: 135

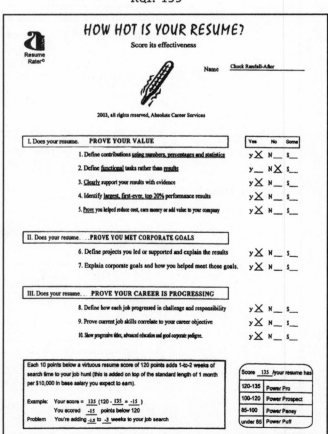

CHUCK RANDALL

2930 Oakwood Lane
Wilmette, IL 60689
847-290-8279

Objective   Currently Socking a position with a progressive company in need of candidates
possessing structural steel, supervisory, safety, and for customer service skills.

Experience
Oct. 78 to
Present   **Ironworkers Local #1 Skokie III Foreman**

General Foreman overseeing the performance of up to 50–60 workers. specific
respon sibilities include hiring, scheduling, planning, monitoring, evaluating,
worker's/project to ensure that Time, Cost, Safety, and Quality goals and
objectives are met. Projects range from shopping malls and buildings 30 stories
in height to erection of steel bridges. Specific technical knowledge included
plumbing, bolting, welding,and detailed revisions as nescssarry. Interaction and
coordination with all interested parties and or stakeholders including federal/state/
and municipal representatives ensuring adherence to all existing & relevant codes,
regulations and statutes. Implemented quality assurance and customer
satisfaction/feedback procedures.

Specific Skills include but arc not limited to

Blue print reading
Welding Mig/Tig, Arc, Combination, overhead, stick , machine
Certified—Load abatement
Certified—HAZMAT
Certified—under OSHA Safety regulations
Certified—Scaffold erection

Education

1.168 to 6/69   Santa Anna College Santa Anna California AAS Degree in Business
Administration

1/70 to 6/71   *Wilson College Chicago III 60612 Business Administration—Acctg*

Additional school information (honors, GPA, etc.)

Personal   Attributes and interests

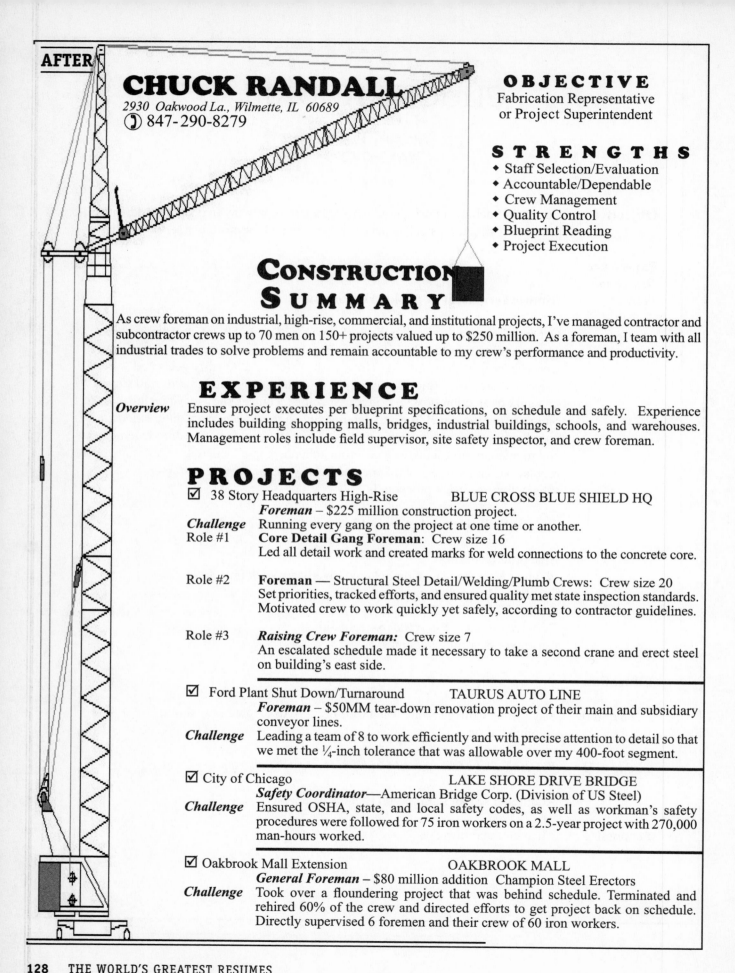

AFTER

CHUCK RANDALL
2930 Oakwood La., Wilmette, IL 60689
☎ 847-290-8279

OBJECTIVE

Fabrication Representative
or Project Superintendent

STRENGTHS
◆ Staff Selection/Evaluation
◆ Accountable/Dependable
◆ Crew Management
◆ Quality Control
◆ Blueprint Reading
◆ Project Execution

CONSTRUCTION SUMMARY

As crew foreman on industrial, high-rise, commercial, and institutional projects, I've managed contractor and subcontractor crews up to 70 men on 150+ projects valued up to $250 million. As a foreman, I team with all industrial trades to solve problems and remain accountable to my crew's performance and productivity.

EXPERIENCE

Overview   Ensure project executes per blueprint specifications, on schedule and safely. Experience includes building shopping malls, bridges, industrial buildings, schools, and warehouses. Management roles include field supervisor, site safety inspector, and crew foreman.

PROJECTS

☑ 38 Story Headquarters High-Rise   BLUE CROSS BLUE SHIELD HQ
   Foreman – $225 million construction project.
Challenge   Running every gang on the project at one time or another.
Role #1   **Core Detail Gang Foreman**: Crew size 16
   Led all detail work and created marks for weld connections to the concrete core.

Role #2   **Foreman** — Structural Steel Detail/Welding/Plumb Crews: Crew size 20
   Set priorities, tracked efforts, and ensured quality met state inspection standards.
   Motivated crew to work quickly yet safely, according to contractor guidelines.

Role #3   ***Raising Crew Foreman:*** Crew size 7
   An escalated schedule made it necessary to take a second crane and erect steel
   on building's east side.

☑ Ford Plant Shut Down/Turnaround   TAURUS AUTO LINE
   Foreman – $50MM tear-down renovation project of their main and subsidiary
   conveyor lines.
Challenge   Leading a team of 8 to work efficiently and with precise attention to detail so that
   we met the ¼-inch tolerance that was allowable over my 400-foot segment.

☑ City of Chicago   LAKE SHORE DRIVE BRIDGE
   Safety Coordinator—American Bridge Corp. (Division of US Steel)
Challenge   Ensured OSHA, state, and local safety codes, as well as workman's safety
   procedures were followed for 75 iron workers on a 2.5-year project with 270,000
   man-hours worked.

☑ Oakbrook Mall Extension   OAKBROOK MALL
   General Foreman – $80 million addition Champion Steel Erectors
Challenge   Took over a floundering project that was behind schedule. Terminated and
   rehired 60% of the crew and directed efforts to get project back on schedule.
   Directly supervised 6 foremen and their crew of 60 iron workers.

Chuck Randall Projects Continued

☑ Downtown Campus   LOYOLA UNIVERSITY
   Foreman—Structural Steel Detail/Plumb Crews: Crew size 20
   Ranken Steel Erection
Challenge Setting priorities, tracked work efforts, ensuring quality met state inspection standards, plumbing, bolting, welding, detail work, and revisions on this 28-story building.

☑ Michigan Avenue Street Bridge   CITY OF CHICAGO
   Foreman—Crew of 7   Pitt Desmoines (PDM)
Challenge A week after leading a team to dismantle and reconstruct the bridge during a total refurbishment, the bridge fell up (one month prior to the opening for the holiday shopping season). Called back to work on the gang, 12–14 hours, 7 days per week to repair the accident in time for Thanksgiving grand opening.

MILITARY   US Marine Corp., S2 Intelligence, Honorable Discharge

CERTIFICATIONS   HAZMAT   OSHA
                      Lead Abatement   Scaffold Erection

EDUCATION   A.A.S., **Business Administration**, Santa Anna College, Santa Anna, CA

——————————————— *References available on request* ———————————————

CHUCK RANDALL'S STORY

Success Snapshot: Construction worker unemployed for fifteen months who lost the use of his left hand from a job accident. Chuck sent his old resume, written by the State Department of Job Security, with 14 typos, to 200 companies—no calls.

Career Sweet Spot: Within six weeks of my rewrite, one of Chicago's two largest construction companies, Walsh, hired him as project superintendent.

Trouble Spot Fixed: He was over fifty-five years old, without a four-year college degree. I positioned him as a supervisor to help him overcome his physical limitations.

To Use This Chart:
1. Score your resume.
2. Find Before and After RQI scores in the PYV, MCG, and CPS categories similar to your scores.
3. Strengthen your weaknesses using our tactics.

BEFORE SCORE		**of 100%**	**Score**
Category I	Prove Your Value	PYV = 0%	0 of 75
Category II	Met Corporate Goals	MCG = 17%	5 of 30
Category III	Career Progress Status	CPS = 50%	15 of 30
	Their RQI Score:	**15%**	**20 of 135**

AFTER SCORE		**of 100%**	**Score**
Category I	Prove Your Value	PYV = 100%	75 of 75
Category II	Met Corporate Goals	MCG = 100%	30 of 30
Category III	Career Progress Status	CPS = 100%	30 of 30
	Our RQI Score:	**100%**	**135 of 135**

CAREER STATS

Career Field:	Construction
Old Title:	Foreman
New Title:	Superintendent
Bridge or Ladder:	Ladder

IMPROVEMENT

From:	Power Puff
To:	Power Pro

KEY

Power Pro:	95% RQI	Power Pansy:	60–80% RQI
Power Prospect:	80–95% RQI	Power Puff:	Below 60% RQI

EILEEN WILKENSON

From a Temp to an Associate Director of Marketing for a Top-5 Consulting Firm

CAREER HIGHLIGHTS

- Total salary increase with our resume: $45,000

- Promotion: From temporary to associate director of marketing

- Job search length: eight weeks

BEFORE
RQI: 45

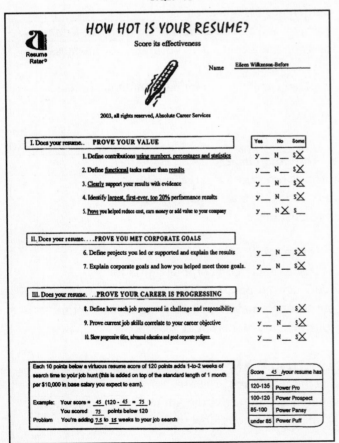

AFTER
RQI: 135

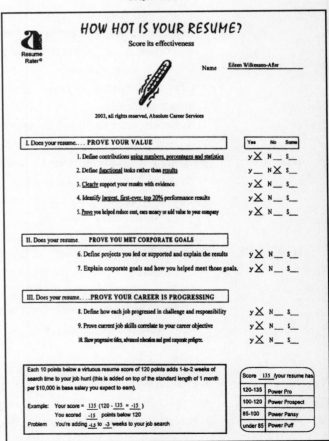

E ILEEN WILKENSON

2895 Worthington Ct. Oak Brook, IL 60308 773-789-3472

EXPERIENCE:

2/00–Present <u>Outsource Marketing</u> **Manpower—Chicago, IL**
- Coordinate logistics of National Restaurant Show booth for Alliant Food Service and Illinois Technology Showcase booth for Andersen Consulting (Ac).
- Write collateral materials, and scripts for Web site demos.
- Manage Web site content for (Ac) dot.com services and Trans World exhibitors products and services.
- Monitor/Implement Marketing Budget for (Ac) Chicago Dot-Corn Launch Centre.
- Support local mCommerce sponsorship programs for (Ac) (i.e. First Tuesday, Wireless Wednesdays, Quarterly Brief Series).
- Provide public relations with city and local newspapers.
- Build relationships with city government (i.e. Mayor Daley Council, IL. Coalition and Chicago Partnership for Economic Development).

4/97–9/99 <u>Marketing Manager</u>, **KPMG—Indianapolis, IN**
- Directed Illinois/NW Indiana Entrepreneur Of The Year® Award. Increased the number of qualified program participants. Promoted Award program through media, presentations to sponsors, target mailings and advertising.
- Coordinated Area Managing Partners team meetings, local IT seminars, regional road shows and Annual International Tax Conference for 600 attendees.
- Managed *Encore Program* of retired partners and served as liaison for the Lake Michigan Area. Utilized retired partner's company contacts to generate new business for Sales Executives.
- Created collateral material for direct mail, ad campaigns, internal communication, and presentations.
- Supervised up to 30 professionals.

2/96–4/97 <u>Freelance Marketing</u>, **SNB Consulting—Indianapolis, IN**
- Designed and wrote the company's business brochure for target mailings.
- Coordinated advisory panels and symposiums for up to 20 participants
- Streamlined questionnaires for client symposiums.

10/95–2/96 <u>Account Manager</u>, **Catholic Charities—Indianapolis, IN**
- Upgraded 6 accounts for the northwest region. Increased corporate gifts for Indianapolis region by 30% and secured 7 new corporate accounts.
- Initiated employee campaigns with new accounts and trained campaign coordinators.
- Managed and developed new campaign strategies for corporate leaders.

9/94–9/95 <u>Assistant Producer/Co-Producer/Talk Show Host</u>, **WNTS Radio—Indianapolis, IN**
- Hosted and produced a Sunday morning public service program.
- Implemented new show ideas and production techniques for the Adrian Rogers Talk Show.
- Revamped national program, "World Watch," with hot global topics.

EILEEN S. WILKENSON
2895 Worthington Ct. Oak Brook, IL 60308 773-789-3472

2/00–present **MANPOWER** **Marketing Consultant** Chicago, IL
Assist clients, such as Andersen Consulting, with structuring and executing marketing programs.

Project **Chicago Dot-Com Launch Centre**—Andersen wants 60% of their revenues to come from Dot Corp. spin-offs (i.e., business segments carved from the Fortune 500) and hope to take up to $1.2 billion in equity within 3 years.

My role Assist two Ac Partners attain the visibility they need to be identified as dot-com market experts. To this end I've secured speaking engagements, sponsorships, city and board appointments.

Project **Wireless Communications**—Andersen is executing a global strategy to be the leader of m-Commerce consulting for wireless and mobile technologies, a market expected to grow from $3.6 billion/FY00 to $140.3 billion by FY05.

My role Support alliances between Ac Partners, Mayor Daley officials (Chicago Partnership for Economic Development), educational institutions (U. of C. and NU's Kellogg business schools), as well as venture capitalists and existing wireless providers.

- Formed a Wireless Roundtable with the Illinois Coalition to establish a common vision of how Chicago can become a wireless Internet innovation center.
- Sponsor m-Commerce programs, i.e., First Tuesday, Wireless Wednesdays, Quarterly Brief Series.

4/97–9/99 **KPMG** **Marketing Manager** Indianapolis, IN
Created collateral material for direct mail, ad campaigns, internal communication, and presentations.

Project **The Entrepreneur of the Year Award**—KPMG's single largest PR strategy to build revenues from a group of 450 consumer product manufacturers and IT/telecommunication companies that earned at least $100 million a year and were based in Illinois/Indiana/Wisconsin.
My role Used media advertising, presentations to sponsors, and target mailings to increase the number of qualified participants by 25% from 420 to 530.

Project **Business Development Using Networked Alliances**—Coordinated IT seminars, regional road shows and annual tax conference for 600 attendees. Managed Encore Program of retired partners. Used partner's company contacts to generate new business for sales executives.

2/96–4/97 **SNB CONSULTING—Managed Care Consulting** **Contract Marketing** Indianapolis, IN
Designed and wrote company brochure, coordinated advisory panels and symposiums.

10/95–2/96 **CATHOLIC CHARITIES** **Account Manager** Indianapolis, IN
Upgraded 6 accounts and secured 7 new corporate accounts, which increased gifts by 30%.

9/94–9/95 **WNTS RADIO** **Coproducer** Indianapolis, IN
Hosted and produced a morning program **Talk Show Host**
Shows • Implemented new show ideas for the Adrian Rogers Talk Show.
• Revamped national program, *World Watch,* with hot global topics.

EDUCATION B.A., Political Science, Loyola University Chicago, IL 1994

EILEEN WILKENSON'S STORY

Success Snapshot: Eileen was a marketing professional on a severe career decline whose most recent job was in a temp role that lasted a year.

Career Sweet Spot: Our resume led to her hire as associate marketing director by Accenture, one of the five largest consulting firms in the United States.

Trouble Spot Fixed: Eileen's career was regressing. I noted her many talents and contributions instead of focusing on her titles.

To Use This Chart:
1. Score your resume.
2. Find Before and After RQI scores in the PYV, MCG, and CPS categories similar to your scores.
3. Strengthen your weaknesses using our tactics.

BEFORE SCORE			of 100%		Score
Category I	Prove Your Value	PYV	=	15%	20 of 75
Category II	Met Corporate Goals	MCG	=	33%	10 of 30
Category III	Career Progress Status	CPS	=	50%	15 of 30
	Their RQI Score:			33%	**45 of 135**

AFTER SCORE			of 100%		Score
Category I	Prove Your Value	PYV	=	100%	75 of 75
Category II	Met Corporate Goals	MCG	=	100%	30 of 30
Category III	Career Progress Status	CPS	=	100%	30 of 30
	Our RQI Score:			100%	**135 of 135**

CAREER STATS

Career Field:	Marketing
Old Title:	Temporary Staffer
New Title:	Marketing Director
Bridge or Ladder:	Ladder

IMPROVEMENT

From:	Power Puff
To:	Power Pro

KEY

Power Pro:	95% RQI	Power Pansy:	60–80% RQI
Power Prospect:	80–95% RQI	Power Puff:	Below 60% RQI

LARENA PAREDO

Dental Hygienist to Sales Associate in Medical Sales

CAREER HIGHLIGHTS

- Salary increase with her new resume: $38,000

- Bridge to pharmaceutical sales

- Job search length: six weeks and moved to a new state of choice

BEFORE

RQI: 20

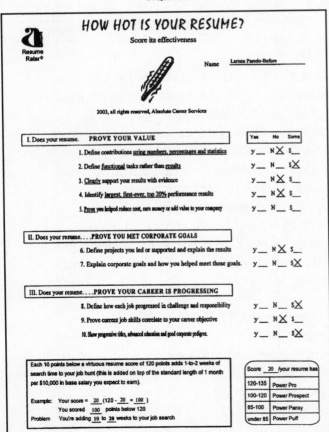

AFTER

RQI: 135

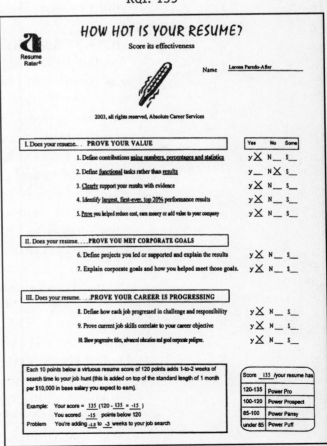

Before and After Resume Examples

LARENA PAREDO
7198 Manchester Drive
Los Angeles, CA 90210
310-687-0127

PROFESSIONAL   Sales Representative Position
OBJECTIVE

EDUCATION   UCLA—Los Angeles, CA
                 Bachelor of Science Degree–Behavioral Science—1995
                 Cal State Fullerton—Fullerton, CA Dental Hygiene Major—
                 1986

WORK
EXPERIENCE   LEE & HARRISON, D.D.S.—Los Angeles, CA
                 August 1995–Present
                 Hygienist—Duties include prophylaxis, intraoral exam
                 using video camera device, patient education on consumer
                 dental products, devices, and medications. Direct contact
                 with customer service representatives such as Oral-B, Butler,
                 Colgate, and Crest to analyze and determine which products
                 best fit the needs of the practice and the patients. Ordering
                 supplies from dental reps.

                 GOOD SAMARITIAN HOSPITAL—Chicago, IL
                 August 1991–August 1995
                 Coordinator of Hygiene Services—Hospital/Clinic setting
                 with fifteen doctors and six residents. An endodontist, an oral
                 surgeon, a pedodontist, two periodontists, several general
                 practitioners and six residents. Good Samaritian is a teaching
                 facility; I was solely responsible for coordinating services,
                 patient care, and scheduling in this busy clinic setting.
                 Attended yearly dental convention to seek out, research,
                 and analyze new products. Developed a strong working
                 relationship and rapport with many dental representatives
                 from several different companies. Responsible for ordering
                 and maintaining adequate and efficient dental products to meet
                 the needs of all our patients.

                 John Roberts, D.D.S. / Gene Grant, D.D.S.
                 September 1986–September 1990
                 Dental Hygienist. All duties included above.

                 REMAX—Fullerton, CA
                 September 1988–September 1990

LARENA L. PAREDO
7198 Manchester Dr., Los Angeles, CA 90210   (310) 678-0127

OBJECTIVE   To sell medical, pharmaceutical, or dental products using existing selling skills that I honed by helping improve revenues and increase patient referrals to make a practice more profitable.

SUMMARY   I've learned that client and patient satisfaction are of the utmost importance. This understanding shapes my professional focus on building strong relationships while handling pressures associated with demanding expectations. Because I have experience in hospitals, clinics, and private practices, where I used my medical background and medical terminology to interact with medical professionals, I am comfortable developing selling relationships with administrative managers as well as individual doctors who make purchasing decisions.

EXPERIENCE
8/95–Present

Hygienist   LEE & HARRISON, D.D.S.   Los Angeles, CA
Overview   See an average of 9 daily patients. I sell prophylaxis and cosmetic dentistry, and educate patients on consumer products, devices, and medications. Analyze and determine which products best fit practice needs with vendor representatives.

STRENGTHS   **Client Management**   Build successful customer relationships that allow me to sell additional services, generate referrals, and ensure client satisfaction.

Sales Assessment   Determine needs and present service options for a wide array of treatment plans that ensure the practice's profitability.

Results
- Average **$22,000** per month in service/product fees.
- Presell cosmetic dentistry treatments costing **$700–$9,600**.
- Close 90% of clients that I recommend buy bleaching kits. This equals 12–16 sales a month at $350 each (**$4,200–$5,600**).
- Sell **$700** deep-cleaning service plans.

8/91–8/95   *Coordinator—Hygiene Services*   GOOD SAMARITAN HOSPITAL   Los Angeles, CA
Overview   Hospital/Clinic with 21 dentists and residents (endodontist, oral surgeon, pedodontist, periodontists, and general practitioners). Since Good Samaritan is a teaching facility, I coordinated services, patient care, and scheduling. Attended conventions to research new products. Developed relations with sales representatives. Ordered and maintained dental products.

Training   Conducted individual assessments of resident's instrumentation techniques.

9/88–9/90   *Sales Associate*   REMAX   Burbank, CA
Overview   Listed, sold, advertised, and created market analysis to sell **$1,000,000** in residential properties. Worked with mortgage, loan officers, and closing agents.

1986   *Pharmacy Technician*   FULLERTON REGIONAL HOSPITAL   Fullerton, CA
Overview   College employment. Intake counselor for patient admissions. Filled prescriptions from doctor orders. Strong communication and organizational skills required.

EDUCATION   B.S., Behavioral Science   **UCLA**   Los Angeles, CA   1995
Dental Hygiene Major   **CAL STATE FULLERTON**   Fullerton, CA   1986

LARENA PAREDO'S STORY

Success Snapshot: Her new resume defined her revenue contribution for the dentist she worked for and made her look like a sales rep.

Career Sweet Spot: Larena became a sales rep initially for Dental Technology Consultants and subsequently for Eli Lilly & Co.

Trouble Spot Fixed: Overcame job lock, a narrowly defined, task-oriented position, and appealed to a medical products/pharmaceutical company.

To Use This Chart:
1. Score your resume.
2. Find Before and After RQI scores in the PYV, MCG, and CPS categories similar to your scores.
3. Strengthen your weaknesses using our tactics.

BEFORE SCORE			of 100%	Score
Category I	Prove Your Value	PYV = 7%		5 of 75
Category II	Met Corporate Goals	MCG = 17%		5 of 30
Category III	Career Progress Status	CPS = 33%		10 of 30
	Their RQI Score:		15%	**20 of 135**

AFTER SCORE			of 100%	Score
Category I	Prove Your Value	PYV = 100%		75 of 75
Category II	Met Corporate Goals	MCG = 100%		30 of 30
Category III	Career Progress Status	CPS = 100%		30 of 30
	Our RQI Score:		100%	**135 of 135**

CAREER STATS

Career Field:	Hygienist to Sales
Old Title:	Hygienist
New Title:	Sales Representative
Bridge or Ladder:	Bridge

IMPROVEMENT

From:	Power Puff
To:	Power Pro

KEY

Power Pro:	95% RQI	Power Pansy:	60–80% RQI
Power Prospect:	80–95% RQI	Power Puff:	Below 60% RQI

JONATHAN HAMPTON

Change to New Industry

CAREER HIGHLIGHTS

• Salary increase with his new resume: $15,000

• Promoted from CSR to ecommerce consultant

• Job search length: eight weeks

BEFORE

RQI: 20

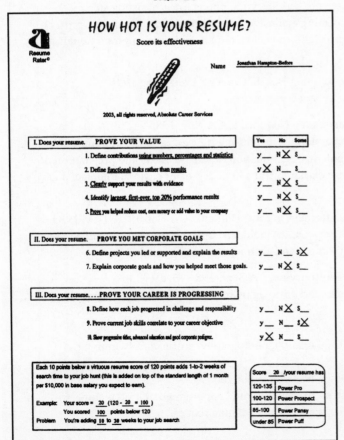

AFTER

RQI: 135

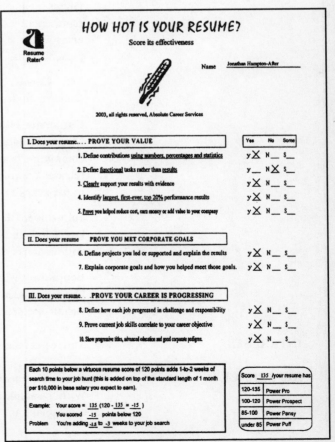

JONATHAN HAMPTON
6774 Michigan Ave., Chicago, IL 60611 312-377-2338

CAREER OBJECTIVE: To utilize my extensive customer oriented skills for the purpose of contributing to the profitability of the company.

EDUCATION: Seattle University, Seattle, WA
Bachelor of Arts in English Writing with a minor in Communication Arts and Sciences, and a minor in Business Administration—May 1987

Representative Courses: Writing of drama, Writing Non-Fiction Prose. Contemporary American Film, Film, Authorship, Literature and Film.

Triton College, River Grove, IL 1982–1984

Lyons Township High School, La Grange, IL 1978–1982

EMPLOYMENT: **California Title Company**, Los Angeles, CA Oct. 1992–Present
Customer Service Representative
Duties Include: Issuance of duplicate title policies and certified mortgage documents, assisting clients with post-closing concerns, working in close contact with the sales department, and a high degree of phone customer contact with occasional in-person calls.

American Title Co., Long Beach, CA June 1991–Sept, 1992
Duties included customer service work, phone sales, assisting sales representatives in locating extensive comparable sales of homes for areas within southern California and Arizona, and making promotional presentations.

West Coast Title Co., Long Beach, CA June 1990–June 1991
Duties included customer service work.

California Title Insurance Co., Irvine, CA Nov. 1985–April 1990
Duties included preparation of the closing figures, assisting in issuing title commitments and policies, examination of release deeds and preparation of releases for county registration and a high degree of customer contact and in-person calls.

Johnson & Block, Attorneys at Law, Burbank, CA Oct. 1983–Nov. 1985
Law Clerk and Courier - Duties included court filings, recording documents with various county offices and abstracting public records.

Benjamin's Mens Shop, Irvine, CA Sept. 1981–Oct. 1983
Duties included stock work, pricing merchandise, and a high degree of customer contact.

INTERESTS: Movies, screen writing, reading, photography, music, and swimming.

REFERENCES: Other references can be furnished upon request.
Writing sample such as six complete and copyrighted motion picture screenplays and other works available upon request.

JONATHAN HAMPTON

274 Fairmont Ave. · Los Angeles, CA 90318
℃ 310-397-2338

OBJECTIVE

To continue in sales where I can contribute to the profitability of a company.

SUMMARY

For ten years, I've built a career where I started in customer service and operational support, to where I am now an account executive and ecommerce consulting professional.

As a *sales professional*, I prospect for new accounts, present our services, and grow business revenues by building relationships with mortgage attorneys, brokers, and bankers.

10/92–2/00	• *Business Developer* **California Title Company,** Los Angeles, CA
Overview	California Title was a new start-up that challenged me to grow our revenue stream immediately or we would go out of business.
Successes	Within 12 months I brought in new clients that grew orders from 0 to 300 per month representing $135,000 in new revenues.
Challenge	In a universe of 2,000 competitors with minimal price differentiation, my clients remained loyal because I made them confident in my sincerity and integrity by remaining accountable to their account expectations.
Sales Results	▸ Won 25 new clients, representing up to $200,000 per month. ▸ Originated 7 of the top 15 accounts. ▸ Won the #1 account worth 20% of all company revenues. ▸ Won back 10 accounts that had left us worth $100K annually.
Unique Duties	▸ Designed print advertisements. ▸ Wrote 2 articles for a trade magazine to market the firm.
Sales Growth	1998 • $2,000,000 1997 • $1,600,000 1996 • $1,000,000

STRENGTHS

- Marketing
- Client Services
- Cold Calling
- Generating Referrals
- Client Retention
- Public Relations
- Business Writing
- Relationship Building

6/91–9/92	• *Customer Service Representative* **American Title Co.,** CA
Overview	Phone sales, assisted sales representatives, and conducted promotional presentations.
6/90–6/91	• *Customer Service Representative* **West Coast Title Co.,** CA
5/87–4/90	• *Title Representative* **California Title Company,** CA
Overview	Prepared closing figures, assisted in issuing title commitments and policies, and prepared releases for county registration. High degree of customer contact and in-person calls.

EDUCATION BA, *English,* Seattle University, Seattle, WA 1987

Technology MS Office, Camtasia Recording, and Video Production/Editing.

References available on request

JONATHAN HAMPTON'S STORY

Success Snapshot: Jon had a flat career. His last four jobs, over fifteen years, were in property title insurance as a customer service representative.

Career Sweet Spot: Hired as an ecommerce consultant for a large dot-com in L.A. He was able to leave a career he disliked and move into the Internet community.

Trouble Spot Fixed: Overcame a career bottleneck in a narrow field by defining his successes, challenges, and results to make him appeal to the Internet community.

To Use This Chart:
1. Score your resume.
2. Find Before and After RQI scores in the PYV, MCG, and CPS categories similar to your scores.
3. Strengthen your weaknesses using our tactics.

BEFORE SCORE			of 100%	Score
Category I	Prove Your Value	PYV =	0%	0 of 75
Category II	Met Corporate Goals	MCG =	17%	5 of 30
Category III	Career Progress Status	CPS =	50%	15 of 30
	Their RQI Score:		**15%**	**20 of 135**

AFTER SCORE			of 100%	Score
Category I	Prove Your Value	PYV =	100%	75 of 75
Category II	Met Corporate Goals	MCG =	100%	30 of 30
Category III	Career Progress Status	CPS =	100%	30 of 30
	Our RQI Score:		**100%**	**135 of 135**

CAREER STATS

Career Field:	ecommerce
Old Title:	CSR
New Title:	Consultant
Bridge or Ladder:	Ladder

IMPROVEMENT

From:	Power Puff
To:	Power Pro

KEY

Power Pro:	95% RQI	Power Pansy:	60–80% RQI
Power Prospect:	80–95% RQI	Power Puff:	Below 60% RQI

VANESSA MARTIN

Librarian Wins Promotion at a Top Library

CAREER HIGHLIGHTS

• Salary raise with new resume: $5,000

• Promotion into a better-funded community library

• Job search length: two weeks

BEFORE
RQI: 15

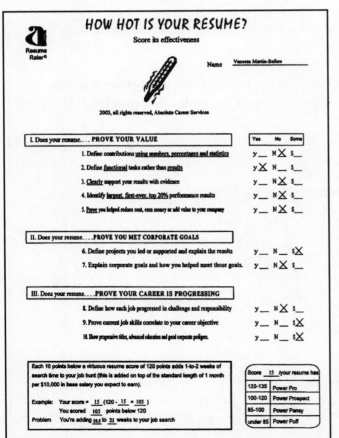

AFTER
RQI: 120

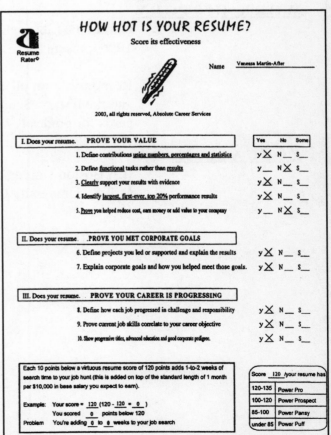

VANESSA MARTIN
2970 Jefferson St.
Boston, MA 02108
617-448-8932

QUALIFICATIONS

- Member ALA
- Member ALSC
- Video reviewer for SLJ
- Library newsletter articles, teacher newsletter
- Bibliographies K-6
- Collection development—juvenile fiction and non-fiction
- Book Discussion group leader
- SRC coordinator
- Teen volunteer coordinator
- Programming—Battle of the Books, library tours
- Write monthly department schedules
- Displays—book and bulletin board

WORK HISTORY

Children's Librarian school Liaison, Sanburg Public library District
1996–present

Responsible for all communications between the area grade schools
and the library. School visits to present booktalks and promote library
cards for grades K-6.

EDUCATION

B.A Boston University, 1995
M.L.S., University Of Massachusetts, 1996

VANESSA MARTIN
2970 Jefferson St. Boston, MA 02108 617-448-8932

OBJECTIVE
To continue a successful career as a children's librarian, in which I can act as the children's reference and reader's advisory resource in order to help them enjoy using their local library.

SUMMARY
I focus on introducing creativity to generate enthusiasm and build patronage for our library by maintaining a contemporary collection that is vibrant, well-organized, and comprehensive. As a professional, I am challenged to meet community expectations for a township that is characterized as highly transitory, multiethnic, and multiracial.

STRENGTHS
- Collection Development
- Creativity
- Public Speaking
- Research
- Student/Teacher Relations
- Writing

EXPERIENCE

Children's Librarian/School Liaison   **SANBURG PUBLIC LIBRARY DISTRICT**
The following topics address a variety of duties, including program development, team management, public relations, planning, and direct marketing to the community.

CHALLENGE 1
BATTLE OF THE BOOKS 1996/1997/1998–present
Manage all PR and organizational planning for this annual program with 7 elementary schools and 125 students reading a list of 63 books. Efforts include conducting 4–5 weekly battles spread over 5 weeks with an awards ceremony, and a guest author whom I invite for up to 150 attendees.
Result   This past season, the 20th anniversary, was a smashing success. The competition was fierce, and the awards ceremony was well received.

CHALLENGE 2
SUMMER READING CLUB
A 2-month program with 1,000+ children participants (preschool to 8th grade). Each year a theme is chosen to capture children's attention so that they read an average of 10 books.
Result   Recruited and managed a volunteer base of 40 young adults, purchased prizes (500 paperbacks), created flyers, and ensured program execution met summer schedule constraints.

CHALLENGE 3
SCHOOL LIAISON – *Book talks, storytelling, story times, group presentations*
Use PR skills as contact point for children to improve their familiarity with the library. Conduct school visits and attend every class between K–6th grades at eight schools, average 210 student presentations a year.
Result   Efforts have successfully built loyal library users among the children.

CHALLENGE 4
COLLECTION DEVELOPMENT
I built Sanburg children's collection, representing a 20% change-over, by evaluating all existing titles, researching reference resources on collection development recommendations, and analyzing popularity of specific books within our consortium of regional libraries.
Result   Properly identified currency, relevancy, and popularity of each classification to have a strong working collection.

Other Duties
Write Library Links, the biannual teacher newsletter, lead library tours, coordinate staff schedules, and write annotated bibliographies for each grade.

EDUCATION
M.L.S., University of Massachusetts Boston, Boston, MA   1996
B.A., Double Major: International Relations & French, Boston University, Boston, MA   1995

VANESSA MARTIN'S STORY

Success Snapshot:	This librarian wanted a higher salary, yet didn't know how to explain what she'd done as a children's librarian to increase patronage at the library. This left her vulnerable to being overlooked as she competed for the one new opening at a nearby library.
Career Sweet Spot:	Defined four key unique contributions that allowed her to win the job offer.
Trouble Spot Fixed:	Elevated an esoteric work history to attract a library's selection board committee.
To Use This Chart:	1. Score your resume.
	2. Find Before and After RQI scores in the PYV, MCG, and CPS categories similar to your scores.
	3. Strengthen your weaknesses using our tactics.

BEFORE SCORE			**of 100%**	**Score**
Category I	Prove Your Value	PYV =	0%	0 of 75
Category II	Met Corporate Goals	MCG =	17%	5 of 30
Category III	Career Progress Status	CPS =	33%	10 of 30
	Their RQI Score:		**11%**	**15 of 135**

AFTER SCORE			**of 100%**	**Score**
Category I	Prove Your Value	PYV =	80%	60 of 75
Category II	Met Corporate Goals	MCG =	100%	30 of 30
Category III	Career Progress Status	CPS =	100%	30 of 30
	Our RQI Score:		**88%**	**120 of 135**

CAREER STATS

Career Field:	Library
Old Title:	Librarian
New Title:	Librarian
Bridge or Ladder:	Lateral — More $

IMPROVEMENT

From:	Power Puff
To:	Power Prospect

KEY

Power Pro:	95% RQI	Power Pansy:	60–80% RQI
Power Prospect:	80–95% RQI	Power Puff:	Below 60% RQI

NATHAN ROCKWELL

Overcame Career Decline

CAREER HIGHLIGHTS

- Salary increase with his new resume: $45,000

- Multiple promotions in under a year

- Job search length: eight weeks

BEFORE

RQI: 85

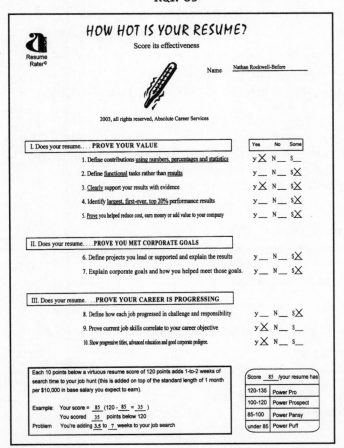

AFTER

RQI: 135

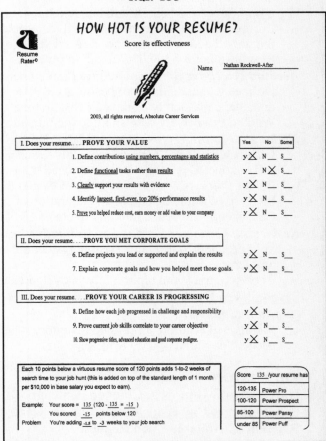

NATHAN ROCKWELL
2217 Lakeland Ave., Northbrook, IL 60648
663-605-2778

OBJECTIVE:

An opportunity to apply my training and experience in sales and marketing to a position offering potential for further professional growth and development.

SUMMARY:

- **A Highly Trained Marketing and Sales Professional**—Academic training combined with extensive hands-on experience in cold calling, telemarketing and referral follow-up resulting in a proven proficiency to consistently expand sales base while ensuring satisfaction of existing clientele.
- **Comprehensive Communication** Skills—Establishes and maintains highly productive relationships with all levels of management and staff personnel.
- **Organizational Abilities Refined through Experience**—Applies time management skills to achieve objectives and ensure the prompt, accurate completion of projects; analyzes problems and quickly implement effective solutions.
- **Computer Literate**—Skilled in Lotus 1-2-3, Paradox, WordPerfect, Windows Applications and other programs.

EXPERIENCE:

SBC Telecommunications, Chicago, Illinois (April 1990–December 1995)

National Accounts Support Consultant (October 1993–December 1995)
- Served as liaison with Montgomery Ward to provide nationwide consultation with telecommunications group; supervised the installation and implementation of telecommunications services.
- Ensured customer satisfaction; resolved problems.
- Suggested additional services as needed.
- Responsible for $500,000/month in revenues.

Account Executive for Branch Sales (September 1992–October 1993)
- Utilized telemarketing, cold calling and referral follow-ups to achieve $5,000/month in new billable revenue; consistently achieved 110% in revenues.
- Worked extensively with small to medium sized businesses.

National Account Representative (March 1991–September 1992)
- Conducted sales of Affinity programs to subsidiaries and affiliates of larger corporate clients; prepared and conducted presentations; interacted with sales and support personnel from companies such as Balcor Property Management, Sara Lee and the Tribune Companies.
- Supervised implementation and operation of services to ensure customer satisfaction.
- Consistently exceeded monthly quota of $3,500 in new revenue.

Residential Customer Service Representative (April 1990–March 1991)
- Sold products to new and existing residential customers by telephone; assisted customers in resolving problems.
- Chosen to track and report daily sales figures for 12 representatives.

Seven Eleven Lombard, Illinois (1985–1990)

Assistant Manager
- Maintained accurate up-to-date inventory of stock for two stores and re-ordered replacement stock as needed; prepared nightly bank deposits.

EDUCATION:

University of Illinois at Chicago, Chicago, Illinois   *M.S. Marketing*   January 1996
Eastern Illinois University, Peoria, Illinois   *B.S. Marketing*   December 1989
References Available Upon Request

NATHAN ROCKWELL

2217 Lakeland Ave. Northbrook, IL 60648 ☎ 663-605-2778

OBJECTIVE　　To pursue a sales career for a technologically innovative company offering a position in which I can help to enhance program development efforts and impact profitability.

EXPERIENCE
1/96–present

Owner/Founder, RHAPSODY INTERIOR, River Forest, IL
Developed and grew a painting business from start-up. Hired and manage a staff of 4 employees, coordinate concurrent projects, negotiate/budget contracts, and foster effective client relations.

4/90–1/96

SBC TELECOMMUNICATIONS, Chicago, IL
National Accounts Consultant　　　　　　　　　　　　　　　　10/93–1/96

As SBC's largest Chicago account, Ward's demanded excellent relationship development and customer service support. The focus was to provide on-site strategic and logistical support by assisting Ward's Executive Telecommunications Staff. Additionally, I was tasked with growing revenues, ensuring telecommunication and technology programs attained objectives, and coordinating SBC's management of Ward's Account Payables and special billing agreements.

Provided nationwide consultation for all telecommunications services (advanced T1s, enhanced call routing, DS3 services, etc.) that generated SBC **$6,000,000** in annual revenues.

Project	National programs to initiate 1-800 Enhanced Call Routing for Ward's Corporate HQ, 500 retail locations, and their Auto Express properties.
Focus	Coordinated installation of new routing services that integrated digital switching and software technologies.
Results	A pilot program beta tested in Chicago with subsequent rollout nationally. SBC generated an additional **$960K** a year.
Project	Ward's new custom executive calling card program.
Focus	Promoted and marketed to Ward's sales and management staffs.
Results	Grew calling card base 260% netting **$210K** in new revenues.

Account Executive for Branch Sales　　　　　　　　　　　　　　9/92–10/93
Implemented sales, marketing, and logistical support efforts.
Focused on selling SBC's service benefits, not price, in order to sell our premium-priced services (up to 100% higher than our competition).
RESULTS: Achieved $5,000/month in new revenue [110% of budgeted goals].

National Account Representative　　　　　　　　　　　　　　　　3/91–9/92
Prepared and made marketing presentations to sell Affinity Programs to subsidiaries and affiliates of large corporations. Clients: Sara Lee, The Tribune Companies.
RESULTS: Consistently exceeded monthly quota of $3,500 in new revenue.

Customer Service Representative　　　　　　　　　　　　　　　　4/90–3/91
Sold products to new and existing residential customers and resolved problems.
Tracked and reported daily sales figures for 12 representatives.

RECOGNITION　　Awarded two Support Representative of the Month Awards.

EDUCATION　　1/96　　**M.S.**　**MARKETING**　　UNIVERSITY OF ILLINOIS AT CHICAGO, Chicago, IL
　　　　　　　　　12/89　　**B.S.**　**MARKETING**　　EASTERN ILLINOIS UNIVERSITY, Charleston, IL

NATHAN ROCKWELL'S STORY

Success Snapshot: Nathan had a masters degree and had even hired another professional resume writer before hiring me, yet couldn't find employment, so he started painting houses.

Career Sweet Spot: His initial job was with Sears. He then came back and was hired by Microsoft. He came back again and was hired by Eaton Corporation.

Trouble Spot Fixed: I developed his work history to attract the Fortune 500 and overcome the stigma of career decline.

To Use This Chart:
1. Score your resume.
2. Find Before and After RQI scores in the PYV, MCG, and CPS categories similar to your scores.
3. Strengthen your weaknesses using our tactics.

BEFORE SCORE			of 100%	Score
Category I	Prove Your Value	PYV =	66%	50 of 75
Category II	Met Corporate Goals	MCG =	33%	10 of 30
Category III	Career Progress Status	CPS =	83%	25 of 30
	Their RQI Score:		**63%**	**85 of 135**

AFTER SCORE			of 100%	Score
Category I	Prove Your Value	PYV =	100%	75 of 75
Category II	Met Corporate Goals	MCG =	100%	30 of 30
Category III	Career Progress Status	CPS =	100%	30 of 30
	Our RQI Score:		**100%**	**135 of 135**

CAREER STATS

Career Field:	Sales
Old Title:	Account Support
New Title:	Project Manager
Bridge or Ladder:	Ladder

IMPROVEMENT

From:	Power Pansy
To:	Power Pro

KEY

Power Pro:	95% RQI	Power Pansy:	60–80% RQI
Power Prospect:	80–95% RQI	Power Puff:	Below 60% RQI

KENT BRADLEY

Policeman to Cellular Tower Negotiator

CAREER HIGHLIGHTS

- Salary increase: $27,000

- From police officer to cellular site negotiator

- Job search length: two weeks

BEFORE

RQI: 20

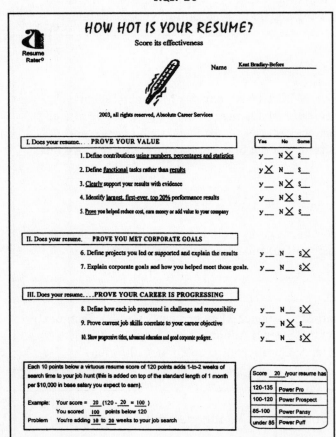

AFTER

RQI: 115

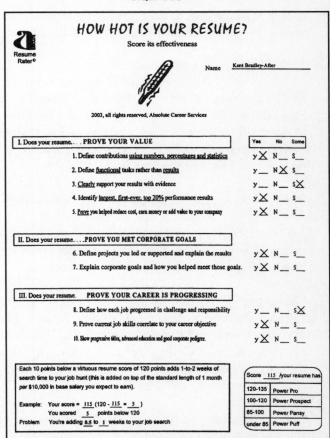

Kent Bradley
2550 Riverview Dr.
Sherman Oaks, CA 91436
818-338-2277

Objective: To become part of a growing organization looking to be an industry leader, that challenges its employees, and rewards for performance.

Employment History

05/97–Present: Burbank, CA
                 Police Officer.
Perform duties of patrol officer for suburb of Los Angeles, which includes initial criminal investigations, report writing, and crime prevention. Certified California Police Officer. Specialized training in Felony Courtroom procedures, criminal investigation, Juvenile relations, and traffic crash investigations.

10/96–Present: New Suburban Reality
                 Realtor (Commercial & Residential)
California licensed Realtor, currently working as a independent sales contractor for a company located in a Los Angeles suburb. Proficient in all aspects of real-estate sales, including commercial and residential sales, leasing, and management.

10/95–05/97:   Home Depot Corporation.
                 Inside Contractor Sales, Department Sales Manager.
Department Sales Manager for custom order Millwork Department of large home improvement retail chain. Duties included interaction with customers on custom order millwork items, requisition of custom orders, management of department employees, merchandising and budgeting for millwork department with gross yearly sales of over 5 million dollars.

11/91–10/95:   United States Navy.
                 Administrative Manager/Technical Specialist.
Enlisted member of the U.S. Navy, with formal training as a Aircraft Maintenance Manager/Technical Specialist on the Sikorsky SH-60F Helicopter. Duties included management of the administrative offices of a aircraft technical school, head of aircraft maintenance, and advisor on technical maintenance and budget director for such school. In addition acted as a recruiter for the time period of 03/95–10/95 for the Navy in the Los Angeles area.

06/90–11/91:   Concord Contractors Corporation.
                 Construction Superintendent.
Job Superintendent for Los Angeles redevelopment corporation. Duties included renovation of multi-family apartment dwellings in low income areas, supervision of all sub-contractors, and assurance of timely completion of all phases of construction.

Education:
*United States Navy Technical Schools, including Aircraft Maintenance Management, Sikorsky Technical Training, Command Assessment Training, Foxbase Computer System Administrator Training, TQM.
*East Los Angeles College Police Academy, Criminal Science/Certificate Completion, California Certified Police Officer.

Special Skills
Computer literate, working knowledge of Windows Operating System. WordPerfect (all editions), most spreadsheets. and Foxbase/Foxpro programming.

KENT A. BRADLEY
2550 Riverview Dr., Sherman Oaks, CA 91436 818-338-2277

OBJECTIVE A position in which I can continue to capitalize on strong analytical, research, and project development skills.

SUMMARY *Since 1990*, employment history covers real estate sales, construction management, contractor sales, and military service. Skills include analyzing developing client relationships, valuating real estate investments, and consulting with owners on construction development. **Market Analysis**: Research economic and real estate indices as well as demographic trends acquired through public and private sources. **Negotiation Skills**: Negotiate lease and sale agreements for commercial properties as well as buyer/seller prices for home mortgages.

REAL ESTATE EXPERIENCE

Commercial Realtor, NEW SUBURBAN REALTY
Overview I've developed prospecting, client management, and marketing skills. Success has been a result of disciplining myself to find opportunities and then persevere until the deal is closed.
Result Sold over $1,000,000 in commercial/residential property sales as well as lease agreements with individual sales of as much as $230,000.

MUNICIPAL EXPERIENCE

Police Officer, BURBANK
Overview Selected out of a pool of 180 applicants (I ranked 10th in the group) to provide policing protection to an exclusive, high-net-worth suburb that includes 3 colleges in a community of 99,000 residents.
Results Received two commendations for outstanding performance.

SALES MANAGEMENT EXPERIENCE

HOME DEPOT CORPORATION
Assistant Department Manager—Contractor Sales
Contractor Sales Coordinator
Overview I played a major role in solidifying relations with Home Depot's core construction customer (general and subcontractor) to mitigate increased competition in our market.
Duties Oversaw a $5,000,000 department, managed a staff of 16 employees, and maintained relationships with 150 vendors. Learned how to specify and analyze blueprints involving electrical, plumbing, hardware, and building materials.
Results Helped store attain #3 status for revenues in 20 stores (#1 for building materials sales). Personal effort allowed me to be promoted to management faster than the entire department.
Project Developed a program to reduce shrinkage (internal/external theft) that saved $20,000/year.

MILITARY EXPERIENCE

US NAVY—HONORABLE DISCHARGE—3 promotions in 4 years
Overview Two months after being assigned to the flight line, I was promoted to handle the role of **QA inspector and technical librarian** of the Aviation Maintenance Training Center. Within 6 months, I became the Administrative Dept. head for 2,000 students and a $14,000,000 annual budget.
Project Coordinated a $35,000,000 change of school focus with a major military vendor, 12-month project. Created a preventative maintenance program that was delivered to the schools' 31 instructors.

CONSTRUCTION DEVELOPMENT EXPERIENCE

Construction Foreman, STANFORD CONTRACTORS CORPORATION
Overview At the age of 19, I led three large-dollar building construction and rehabilitation projects: 46 units, 21 units, and 18 units, respectively.
Duties Coordinated as many as 30 subcontractors (HVAC, Plumbing, Dry Wall, Flooring, Electrical) for up to 8-month projects. Oversaw budgets of up to $500,000.

EDUCATION Navy Tech Schools (Aircraft Maintenance and Computer System Maintenance)

KENT BRADLEY'S STORY

Success Snapshot: This police officer didn't want to give tickets based on a quota system, so he wanted to leave the police force.

Career Sweet Spot: After he faxed his new resume, he was hired, sight unseen, by a Florida-based company. They made him their West coast cellular tower negotiator and gave him $6,000 more than he was earning. Within three months, two other cellular companies hired him and added another $21,000 in salary.

Trouble Spot Fixed: No experience in cellular communications and no tangible experience in negotiations.

To Use This Chart:
1. Score your resume.
2. Find Before and After RQI scores in the PYV, MCG, and CPS categories similar to your scores.
3. Strengthen your weaknesses using our tactics.

BEFORE SCORE			of 100%	Score
Category I	Prove Your Value	PYV = 0%		0 of 75
Category II	Met Corporate Goals	MCG = 33%		10 of 30
Category III	Career Progress Status	CPS = 33%		10 of 30
	Their RQI Score:		15%	**20 of 135**

AFTER SCORE			of 100%	Score
Category I	Prove Your Value	PYV = 87%		60 of 75
Category II	Met Corporate Goals	MCG = 100%		30 of 30
Category III	Career Progress Status	CPS = 83%		25 of 30
	Our RQI Score:		88%	**115 of 135**

CAREER STATS

Career Field:	Sales
Old Title:	Police Officer
New Title:	Aquisition Specialist
Bridge or Ladder:	Bridge & Ladder

IMPROVEMENT

From:	Power Puff
To:	Power Prospect

KEY

Power Pro:	95% RQI	Power Pansy:	60–80% RQI
Power Prospect:	80–95% RQI	Power Puff:	Below 60% RQI

EDWARD BAILEY

Promotion to IT Manager

CAREER HIGHLIGHTS

• Salary increase with his new resume: $20,000

• Promoted to database manager

• Job search length: three months

BEFORE
RQI: 40

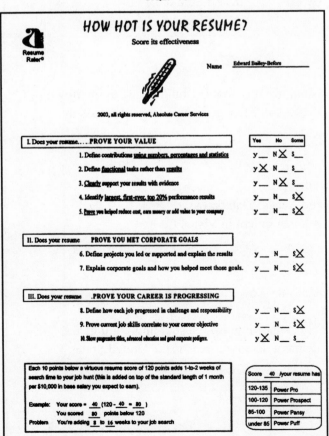

AFTER
RQI: 125

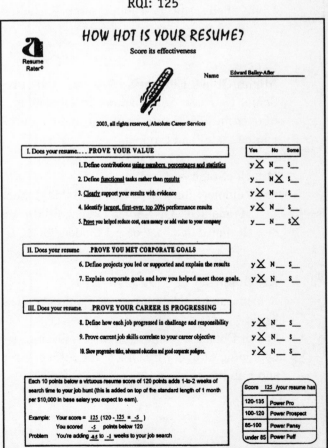

Ed Bailey
2890 Sunset Dr., Oak Park, IL 60301 708-512-1422

Summary

Progressive database technology experience in the asset management, publishing, and alternative media fields. Capable of directing multiple projects and implementing emerging technologies under tight deadlines. Management skills encompass supporting organizational business units and integrating complex information systems. Network with technical staff, executive officers and end-users to attain the twin goals of delivering solutions while hitting revenue/cost targets.

Skills

SQL Server 7.0 and 2000; Oracle 8.0 NT and Solaris (database maintenance, migration, Q.C.)
Autopagination in Quark XPress, Xyvision, Frame, Interleaf Word, and Excel
Oracle Pro C Precompiler, PL/SQL (Embedded SQL)   PowerBuilder
UNIX (Sun Solaris, IBM AIX and SGI IRIX)   Visual C++ Foundation Classes
Windows NT and 2000 (GCI / Java Script)   Gnu C++ programming/debugging
UNIX shell scripts (C-shell, Bourne, K-shell, Perl, BASh) Install Shield 6.1

Experience
Mirim/Quark Enterprise Systems 3/98–Present
Senior Database Administrator in developing, supporting, troubleshooting, tuning, and upgrading of over thirty SQL Server eStage and Oracle QuarkDMS Asset Management databases across the United States and Europe.

Quark eStage
- Remotely Supported Customers' SQL Server Databases.
- Maintained SQL Server, Oracle, FileMaker Pro and Access Databases.
- Designed database object models for SQL Server development in Visual C++.

RR Donnelley & Sons 8/90–2/98
Senior Database Administrator, Senior Applications Analyst - Powerbase Technology Group @ Coris
Senior Database Administrator (overseeing staff of 3) in supporting, troubleshooting, tuning, and upgrading of over fifty Oracle Interoffice Asset Management databases across the United States and Europe.

Ed Bailey

RRD Projects:
Cons Publisher Gateway
- Tuned application for an 80% improvement in database access rate.
- Developed reports for production to monitor database growth.
- Designed database object models for parallel Java and PowerBuilder development.

National Semiconductor Web Prototype
- Wrote SQL scripts to confirm data integrity after migration from IBM mainframe to Oracle.
- Resolved a 2 month schedule bottleneck within 3 weeks of assignment.

Content Delivery Service
- Designed and implemented the database auto processing Agent template (used in all subsequent customer specific agents).
- Main consultant on using Agents to extend Oracle Asset Management database functionality.
- Implemented auto processing of check-in to oversee customized server processing from Oracle.
- Created database scripts to load the Expanded Oracle Interoffice Asset Classes.
- Wrote PL/SQL subroutines to Expand API access to auxiliary tables.
- Coordinated with Production Services when designing workflow for automated processes.

Output Planner Prototype
- Team supervisor of the GUI programming (staff of 4).
- Coordinated with Publisher Gateway Team to develop extendible products.

Yellow Pages
- Wrote programs to determine and eliminate 90% of pagination, proofing and typesetting errors.

Maintained Donnelley Composition System
- Designed and implemented work flow improvements to reduce hand work, remakes, and reprints.

DCS Output In Postscript
- Made changes necessary to allow migration from Video Comp proprietary format to Postscript.

Savings & Community Banks Assoc., CD ROM From Xyvision Files
- Supervised programming. Project was 6 months behind schedule when management gave me the lead of the project. Within 4 months we had completed it on-time and under budget by consolidating three project teams to eliminate redundant work.

GEC Plessey
- Output in NSC CD ROM format from document database. This became the prototype design of the Publisher Gateway Asset Management System.

Wallace Computer Services 7/80–8/90
Senior Systems Consultant, Database Publishing—Wallace Press Division
Main technical liaison between sales staff and customers to ensure schedule and delivery compliance.
Responsible for project designs, programming, system administration and vendor contact.

Maremont Muffler and Midas Muffler Catalogs and Price Lists
- Wrote programs to generate regional and specialty price lists from a single database.
- Wrote a program to generate labels and work flow steps for best shipping prices, shipping UPS by zone and USPS bulk rate discounts.
- Designed copy mark up and tagging for price merge from database into catalog pages.

Education   Illinois Institute of Technology
BA, Computer Science, *with Honors*   Minors: Math & Physics
- Teacher's Aide at IIT for Assembly Language and Computer Architecture Courses.

ED BAILEY

2890 Sunset Dr., Oak Park, IL 60301 708-512-1422

Objective   Database Administrator or project development manager in an Oracle/SQL Server environment.

Experience
- **Supervised**   Team of 4 DBA's
- **3 years**   SQL Server DBA in development and beta site environments
- **5 years**   Oracle DBA in both production/development environments.
- **10 years**   Oracle Development using MS Visual Studio, C++, Java, PowerBuilder and PL/SQL in Win NT/2000 and UNIX (Sun Solaris, IBM AIX and SGI IRIX) environments.

3/98 - Present   **Senior Database Administrator**   QUARK INC.

Overview ...   Recruited by the Chairman of the Board and the VP of Client Server Development as part of the purchase agreement when Quark Inc. bought *Coris Publisher*™ from RR Donnelley (which I was instrumental in developing).

Focus 1   To migrate *Coris Publisher*™ to an Oracle based *QuarkDMS*™ (Digital Media System).

Purpose   *QuarkDMS*™ positions Quark as the dominant solution provider for digital publishing in the enterprise and as a knowledge management tool for digital related assets. *QuarkDMS*™ nets $100,000 per site.

Focus 2   While continuing to develop *QuarkDMS*™, I became part of the global product launch team tasked with developing *Quark eStage*™, an application that leverages Quark's presence in Digital Publishing and helps Quark dominate Catalog Publishing and Publish-to-Web markets.

Purpose   *Quark eStage*™ is a client/server system for database-driven publishing for retail, B-2-B and B-2-C catalog and direct marketing. It can reduce the cycle time of strategy-to-promotion up to 75% by linking the merchandising process to the advertising department. *Quark eStage*™ is sold at $125,000 per site.

Final Impact   At $100,000 and $125,000 per contract, Quark expects my two products to earn $40.25MM in near-term revenues, primarily by selling to Global 1000 corporations and then by penetrating the broader market place with eventual roll-in to the flagship QuarkXpress application.

My roles

DBA work
- Maintained development databases in Oracle, SQL Server, FileMaker Pro and Access.
- Environment Oracle 8.0 NT and Sun Solaris; SQL Server 7.0 and 2000 Win NT/2000.
- Cloned and defragmented databases using DTS and VB Script.
- Supported and tuned SQL Server OLTP and OLAP databases traveling to client site as needed.
- Data warehouse using star schema, data load, data transformation, mining, and OLAP cubes.

DB Design
- UML models for SQL Server development in Visual C++ using Rational Rose CASE tool.
- Designed the database architecture, set up standards, and performed capacity planning.
- Developed GCI forms and Java Scripts for automated project build and distribution.
- Retrofitted databases; performed table modifications and schema changes to engineer solutions.
- Mentored programmers on database access methods and heterogeneous joins using Rogue Wave.
- Wrote DMO program for creating SQL Server Databases using Install Shield 6.1.

8/90 – 2/98   **Senior Database Administrator, Sr. Applications Analyst**   RR DONNELLEY & SONS

Overview ...   Original purpose was to open access to data for key customers by migrating Donnelley's 35 year old proprietary DCS publishing system from the IBM mainframe platform to an Oracle-Sun client server environment. Since the migration included using standard desk top publishing tools such as Quark Xpress, we were far along the development curve to creating a robust Asset/Knowledge Management product Donnelley could sell to business customers.

Focus   Full cycle development of *Coris Publisher*™, an Oracle based DMS (Digital Media System) which acts as a central repository for digital publishing-related assets, i.e. text files, graphics, photos, movies and sound. Powerfull query features allow users to search for shared assets using keywords, dates, and file types. The system features state-of-the-art security.

Purpose   Every word, layout, photo and graphic an organization produces is immediately accessable and can be used directly from each staff member's desktop.

Final Impact   The success of this product led to Quarks eventual purchase.

My roles

DBA work
- Maintained Production, Development and Customer's Oracle databases.
- Environment Oracle 7.0 thru 8.0 in UNIX (Sun Solaris, IBM AIX and SGI IRIX) and Win NT.
- Upgraded Oracle Databases in a 24/7 environment (traveled to client sites as needed).
- Used Oracle Enterprise Manager to monitor databases (used performance pack and diagnostics tool options).
- Developed automated monitoring reports that provided early warning trouble spots: extents, space and performance concerns, detect fragmentation, inefficient access, high-level server resource management, replication, index and tablespace utilization.
- Set up Queries to page DBA when a production database went down.
- Tuned application, which improved the database access rate by 80%.
- Performed cold and hot backups, data recovery, point-in-time recovery and disaster recovery using Legato Storage Manager.
- Developed and implemented security models, assigning database roles and privileges.
- Developed and maintained UNIX shell scripts for installing database, building user defined data types, and creating schemas (C-shell, Bourne, Korn-shell, Perl, BASh).

Management
- Supervised, mentored, and trained other DBA's.
- Conducted performance reviews.
- Prioritized multiple tasks between Production, Development and Systems departments.

DB Design
- Designed database constraints to ensure integrity of the database instances.
- Full life-cycle experience from requirements gathering through logical and physical modeling, design, development, testing, initial parameter settings, implementation, database capacity requirements, space forecasting, and tuning.
- Designed ERD database object models for parallel Java and PowerBuilder development using ERWIN CASE tool.
- Implemented RAID configuration for high availability, maximum performance and reliability.
- Mentored application programmers for improving the efficiency of their SQL code.
- Initialized tables and ConText server cartridge using SQL*Loader scripts.
- Wrote SQL scripts to facilitate migration from IBM mainframe to Oracle.
- Distributed databases, snapshots, replication, table partitioning and Oracle Parallel Server.
- Database publishing in Quark XPress, XML, HTML, Xyvision, Frame, Interleaf, Word, and Excel.

- **5/81 - 8/90 Senior Systems Consultant** **WALLACE COMPUTER SERVICES**

Overview..... Main technical liaison between sales staff and customers to ensure schedule and delivery compliance as well as maintaining plant operating capacity. Responsible for design, programming, system administration and vendor contact.

Education
9/73 - 5/81 **Illinois Institute of Technology**
BA, *with Honors*, Computer Science   Math & Physics
Teacher's Aide at IIT for Assembly Language and Computer Architecture Courses.

EDWARD BAILEY'S STORY

Success Snapshot: A technology professional caught in the worst tech employment market in fifty years, Ed was fired before the software product he had worked on for three years was launched.

Career Sweet Spot: His new resume found him work for UBS Paine Webber that paid him a higher salary. Without experience in the financial industry, Ed was hired, given a raise, and assigned to manage more staff than he had led before, all within three months of hiring us.

Trouble Spot Fixed: Helping a mid-fifties professional in a down job market earn a six-figure salary in a new industry.

To Use This Chart:
1. Score your resume.
2. Find Before and After RQI scores in the PYV, MCG, and CPS categories similar to your scores.
3. Strengthen your weaknesses using our tactics.

BEFORE SCORE			of 100%	Score
Category I	Prove Your Value	PYV =	13%	10 of 75
Category II	Met Corporate Goals	MCG =	33%	10 of 30
Category III	Career Progress Status	CPS =	67%	20 of 30
	Their RQI Score:		**30%**	**40 of 135**

AFTER SCORE			of 100%	Score
Category I	Prove Your Value	PYV =	87%	65 of 75
Category II	Met Corporate Goals	MCG =	100%	30 of 30
Category III	Career Progress Status	CPS =	100%	30 of 30
	Our RQI Score:		**93%**	**125 of 135**

CAREER STATS

Career Field:	Technology
Old Title:	Database Admin.
New Title:	Sr. Database Admin.
Bridge or Ladder:	Ladder and Bridge

IMPROVEMENT

From:	Power Puff
To:	Power Prospect

KEY

Power Pro:	95% RQI	Power Pansy:	60–80% RQI
Power Prospect:	80–95% RQI	Power Puff:	Below 60% RQI

FREDERICK TAYLOR

Multiple Promotions in Banking

CAREER HIGHLIGHTS

- Salary increase with his new resume: $77,000

- Promoted to VP of a large National Bank

- Job search length: seamless

BEFORE

RQI: 55

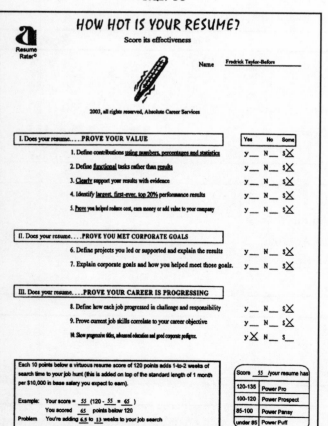

AFTER

RQI: 125

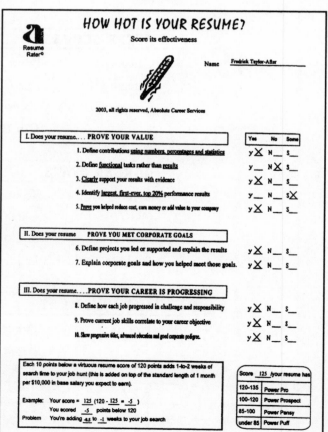

FREDERICK TAYLOR

4578 Wellington Avenue, Hoffman Estates, IL 60330 (312) 798-3446

SUMMARY

Ten years experience in the U.S. and foreign financial services industry including financial analysis, strategic planning, accounting and general management skills for investment products. Maintain consistent record of leadership, minimizing and reducing costs, improving productivity through leveraging technology and team building.

PROFESSIONAL EXPERIENCE

NationsBanc Chicago, IL   **(1988–1998)**

Vice President, Equities   **1996–Present**

Manage foreign and domestic stock equities team of 10 overseeing profit and loss analysis totaling profits of $35MM. Direct team, workflow and daily assignments and quality assurance of products.

- Maintain department budget totaling over $ 1MM.
- Interview, hire, train and conduct salary and performance reviews.
- Interact with traders, interpreting and implementing requests and system support for products in New York, Chicago, Tokyo, Singapore, Hong Kong, Frankfurt, London, Switzerland.
- Troubleshoot and produce solutions as application and systems expert for option rates, market opinion values, option values and position reporting.
- Work directly with technical team to make computer application modifications.
- Organize secure electronic and hard copy back-up routines for equities, interest rate products and foreign exchange and energies groups' statistical and theoretical files.
- Assist with special issues involving human resources, off-shift security, holiday coverage, automation and trader relations.

Senior Financial Analyst, U.S. and Foreign Equities Team   **1994–1996**

Provided profit and loss analysis and UNIX system reporting for stock index products nationally and internationally. Acted as liaison for alterations to statistical and financial reports.

- Designed macro alterations for p&l for S&P's, German stocks and DAX, London FTSE and Swiss SMI.
- Facilitated task forces orchestrating office relocation, developing automated computer and manual checking processes and creating and implementing an education program.
- Coordinated corporate disaster recovery program covering data and physical facility relocation for 50 persons.

Financial Analyst, Cash Management and Margins   **1991–1994**

- Generated reports for senior management in all trading areas.
- Updated cash management and out-of-pocket analysis, margin reporting, margin predicting programs, trade accounting and position reports.
- Assured proper trade and account allocation with back office for trade accounting.
- Developed computer-based predicting and calculating tools with the technical programming team.

Trade Support Analyst, Foreign Exchange and Precious Metals 1989–1991
- Supported currency and metals markets including: British pound, Canadian and Australian dollars, German mark, Swiss franc, gold, silver, platinum and copper.
- Interacted daily with U.S. and foreign traders producing all reporting requests.

Trade Support Analyst, Interest Rate Products 1988–1989
- Produced reports for Euro Dollar, 30, 10 and 5 year U.S. Bonds and T-Notes market areas.

Clerk, at the Chicago Board of Options Exchange S&P 500. 1988

COMPUTER SKILLS

Faxworks PRO LAN Email
Quatro Pro Workgroups

UNIX and DOS Operating Systems
Microsoft Excel and Word

EDUCATION AND TRAINING

Cornell University Ithaca, NY
   Bachelor of Arts, Social Science
NationsBank
   Options theory classes and hands on training. 1988–1998
   Managing Your Development 1997

CIVIC ACTIVITIES

Board Commission Deacon, Property and Finance Commission Member, Chairman of Missions Committee, Treasurer and foreign support of volunteer medical teams.

FREDERICK E . TAYLOR
4578 Wellington Avenue, Hoffman Estates, IL 60330 (312) 798-3446

■ EXPERIENCE ■

| 11/98–present | *V.P. Capital Markets* | **BANKONE**, Chicago, IL |

Hired in 1998 as the VP of Capital Markets for First Chicago and then transitioned to BankOne at the merger. *The key challenge* is managing a staff of 12 trade valuation, P&L, and risk analysts who track profitability of the bank's trading strategies in 3 business areas: Commodities, Equities, and International Interest Rates. BankOne, since my hire, increased trading revenues from $22MM to $75MM (or 340%).

PROJECT

SYSTEMS MIGRATION & UPGRADE

Devon ⇨ Globe Conversion — Led team of 9 to convert the trade valuation phase of a management reporting tool that tracks asset values, payments, and other accounting data on trading activities.
Result   Although front/back offices rolled out their phases over 14 weeks, my component (middle office) was implemented error free (per internal audit) in 2 weeks.

ComSwap ⇨ Murex: Member of conversion team and leader of a 2-person group tasked with migrating an in-house commodity tracking system.
Result   Implemented system under 50% of projected time frame as budgeted by Murex systems consultant.

PROJECT

CONSOLIDATION OF LONDON OPERATIONS

Teamed with the SVP of trading and SVP of operations & planning to streamline the derivatives operations of the London division. This included adding UK staff to my team for a year-long transition period as well as hiring 15 new staff to replace them upon their exit.
Result   Project is in process, but will save BankOne $4MM annually.

PROJECT

BANKONE & FIRST CHICAGO MERGER INTEGRATION

Teamed with the VP of IT to ensure front office and accounting operations continuity during conversion of BankOne's trading operations to FirstChicago's system.
Result   Project success is evidenced by a negligible amount of postconversion issues.

| 1988–1998 | **BANK OF AMERICA**, Chicago, IL | |
| | *V.P.—Equities* | 1996–1998 |

Overview   Originally hired by Chicago Research & Trading in 1988 as an analyst until CRT was acquired by NationsBank in 1995. A year later I was promoted to VP and managed a team of 10 trade analysts, a $1MM department budget, oversaw hiring, training, and staff performance reviews. *The key challenge* was leading staff to stress test market trading scenarios for NYC, Chicago, Tokyo, Singapore, Hong Kong, Frankfurt, London, and Swiss branches. The team also conducted P&L and risk analysis on a book of business that generated **$35MM in annual profits**.

PROJECT

MANAGER FOR IT & TRADING OPERATIONS DEPARTMENTS

Worked with IT to create or modify reports on option rates.
Result   Created a new market opinion value reports and trading position report.

Senior Financial Analyst, U.S. & Foreign Equities Team   1994–1996
Overview   Analyzed P&L for national and international stock index products. Designed computer models on the S&P, German, UK, and Swiss exchanges. Developed automated checking processes.

Frederick Taylor

Overview

Financial Analyst, Cash Management & Margins   1991–1994
Updated cash management analysis, margin reporting/predicting programs, trade accounting, and position reports. Assured proper trade and account allocation with back office. Developed computer-based predicting and calculating tools with the technical programming team.

Overview

Trade Support Analyst, Foreign Exchange and Precious Metals   1989–1991
Supported currency and precious metals markets, i.e., British pound, Canadian and Australian dollars, German mark, Swiss franc, gold, silver, platinum, and copper.

Overview

Trade Support Analyst, Interest Rate Products   1988–1989
Reported on Euro Dollar, 30-, 10-, and 5-year U.S. bonds and T-Notes market areas.

EDUCATION

Cornell University   B.A., Social Science
NationsBank   Commodity Options theory classes

CIVIC

Treasurer, not-for-profit entity based in Lesotho, South Africa. The primary focus is to train the unemployed in how to run a trade business in fields such as carpentry and sewing.

References available on request

FREDERICK TAYLOR'S STORY

Success Snapshot: Initially Fred hired me to teach him salary negotiations, which led to a $37,000 salary increase ($15,000 over initial offer). A year later he hired me to write his resume, which led to a job with a large bank and $40,000 more.

Career Sweet Spot: He wanted more money. He went from $43,000 to $120,000 in two years.

Trouble Spot Fixed: We needed to correlate his background in investments to fit the banking industry.

To Use This Chart:
1. Score your resume.
2. Find Before and After RQI scores in the PYV, MCG, and CPS categories similar to your scores.
3. Strengthen your weaknesses using our tactics.

BEFORE SCORE				**of 100%**	**Score**
Category I	Prove Your Value	PYV	=	33%	25 of 75
Category II	Met Corporate Goals	MCG	=	33%	10 of 30
Category III	Career Progress Status	CPS	=	67%	20 of 30
	Their RQI Score:			**41%**	**55 of 135**

AFTER SCORE				**of 100%**	**Score**
Category I	Prove Your Value	PYV	=	87%	65 of 75
Category II	Met Corporate Goals	MCG	=	100%	30 of 30
Category III	Career Progress Status	CPS	=	100%	30 of 30
	Our RQI Score:			**93%**	**125 of 135**

CAREER STATS

Career Field:	Finance to Banking
Old Title:	VP Trade Support
New Title:	VP Business Planning
Bridge or Ladder:	Ladder

IMPROVEMENT

From:	Power Puff
To:	Power Prospect

KEY

Power Pro:	95% RQI	Power Pansy:	60–80% RQI
Power Prospect:	80–95% RQI	Power Puff:	Below 60% RQI

PHILLIP LANGDON

HR Trainer Joins an International Engineering Company

CAREER HIGHLIGHTS

- Salary increase with his new resume: $5,000+

- Hired by a German company

- Job search length: twelve weeks

BEFORE

RQI: 30

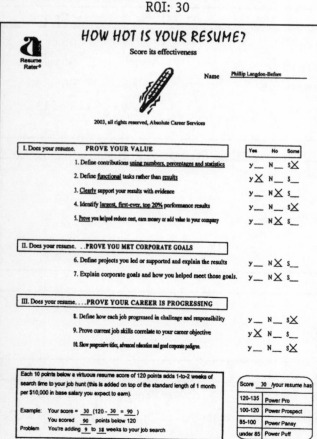

AFTER

RQI: 135

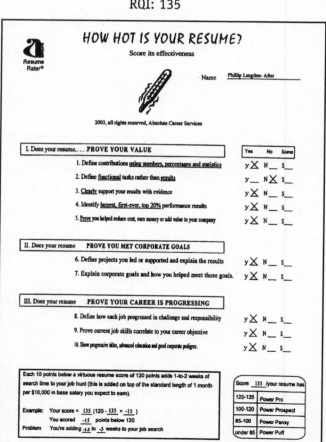

PHILLIP P. LANGDON
312-449-2689, 235 Lakeshore Drive   Chicago, IL 60622

Objective: I will provide your business with for the personal and professional development using cutting edge training technologies and methodologies

Leadership
- Managed Part time Instructor Program of 40 instructors which support two locations that provide training for 7,000 employees annually.
- Served as Dale Carnegie Graduate Assistant.
- Awarded three instructors for outstanding service.
- Responsible for personal and professional development of full and part time instructors.
- Master Trainer for Interpersonal skill workshops.
- Conduct monthly meetings for 40 part-time instructors
- Aviation Hydraulic Shop Supervisor with 9 Direct Reports in support of a Squadron of 12 aircraft.
- Certified to authorize aircraft safe-for flight
- Completed Non Commissioned Officer Training

Communication
- Instruct/Facilitate five technical workshops
- Instruct/Facilitate five interpersonal skill workshops
- Instruct/Facilitate 4 quality workshops
- Developed two On-the Job training programs
- Developed two classroom training workshops
- Developed Instructor Satisfaction Assessment
- Provide instructor evaluation Feedback for 40 part-time instructors and 9 internal instructors
- Designed and conducted an instructor audit of 300 instructors
- Worked with associates to develop a worldwide Instructor Certification Program
- Developed certification test for 300 Distribution employees
- Trained personal in aviation maintenance

Planning and organizing
- Established Instructor Guidelines
- Facilitated interdepartmental training needs analysis
- Developed and initiated Part-time instructor interview process
- Developed and implemented instructor satisfaction assessment
- Ensured training needs were provided by rescheduling or providing additional training events to meet customer needs
- Facilitated meeting to revise Instructor database from Chicagoland area to provide service to Nokia University Midwest Region
- Received Letter Of Commendation from the Secretary of the Navy for completing repair of several aircraft with limited resources during wartime conditions

Education
 University of Texas at Austin
 - B.S. Business Management , 2001

Nokia University
 - TTT Instructor 101 1997

Langevin Learning Services
 - Instructional Design 1996
 - Training Needs Analysis 1996
 - Technical Writing 1997
 - Marketing Your Training 1997
 - Advanced Instructional Design 1998

Employment History
Instructor/Instructional Designer, Nokia University 1998–Present

Instructor/Instructional Designer, Nokia Cellular Subscriber Sector 1996–1998

Aviation Hydraulic Pneumatic Specialist, United States Marine Corps 1983–1991

PHILLIP P. LANGDON
912-449-2689, 235 Lakeshore Drive   Irving, TX 75060

10/93–present	**NOKIA**	**Irving, TX**	
	7/98–present	Instructor/Instructional Designer III	Nokia University
	2/96–7/98	Instructor/Instructional Designer I	Nokia Cell Subscriber Sector
	11/92–2/96	Cellular Operator	Cellular Subscriber Group

Overview   My initial technical role lasted 3 years, as I supported a project with LA Cellular. At LA Cellular, I created and delivered *The Defects in Manufacturing Analysis Report* to our divisional VP and entire manufacturing staff. This led to becoming a part-time instructor and training coordinator until 1996, when I was promoted to a full-time instructor/instructional designer.

My Impact   Since 1996 I've saved $1,000,000 by developing courses from scratch or tailoring existing courses to fit needs. I've delivered 15 courses and designed 18 training solutions, a total of 2000 training hours spread over 265 classes for a student population of 7500.

Areas Taught
- Human Relations
- Middle Management
- Interpersonal Skills
- Technology
- Distribution
- Quality Programs
- Engineering Software and R&D
- Manufacturing Initiatives

Project Focus   Delivered a 2-day course on continuous improvement strategies to our Hong Kong manufacturing site, Asian HQ for semiconductor products. Course focused on statistical process control [SPC] and problem-solving methods delivered to 14 lead engineers (Black Belt Engineers).
Actions   To enable engineers to teach their staff how to reduce product development cycle time while improving the production reliability yield in semiconductor manufacturing.
Result   Reliability yield is projected to increase from 93% to 99.999% (five-9s reliable).

Project Focus   Member of project team of 5 who redesigned an ATSO program (Applied Technologies Software Organization) for Nokia's use to train 1,800 personal communications software engineers.
Actions   Nokia needed new course material (8 sessions and 43 modules) developed in a reduced timeline of 4 weeks from the original 12-week schedule. I modified instructor and participant guides as well as redesigned the PowerPoint presentation.
Result   Personally created 3 of 8 sessions with 18 individual modules. Overall we saved Nokia $25,000 and 150 engineering man hours (at $30/hr).

Project Focus   Create new training for Global Distribution Ctr: 40 technicians; 2MM units shipped per month.
Actions   Identified 15 areas of training need and developed training roadmap for 13 OJT solutions of which I implemented 5. Found 2 existing Nokia University courses, which saved 16 weeks of development time, and found vendor to deliver courses.
Result   The structured training program brought the department into ISO 9000 compliance.

Project Focus   Client needed electrostatic discharge training for 250 pick & pack distribution employees.
Actions   Modified an existing 8-hour course into a 2-hour module (saving 1,500 productivity hours) and met with quality and production line managers to ensure their commitment.
Result   Turned the 2-hour module into an I³ e-learning solution delivered on both CD-rom and Internet link; overall this will eliminate lost line productivity.

Project Focus   Nokia relocated a major portion of manufacturing from the United States to Chihuahua, Mexico.
Actions   Consulted with Chihuahua Nokia University Manager on how to use the web-based OJT library database as a key resource to train 800 manufacturing operators.
Result   Chihuahua now produces 15% of all hand sets or 3.6 million units to U.S. standards.

Project Focus

Phase 1	Training on a new European product packaging methodology (Paceline system).
Actions	Created 8-hour course with classroom activity, assembly line training, and 30-minute video delivered to 250 line employees.
Result	Production rates increased by 25% from 1200 units to 1500 units.

Phase 2	Client needed course time reduced and increased availability of course schedules.
Actions	Redesigned course from 8 to 4 hours, implemented a monitored OJT program as follow-up, and trained 6 distribution personnel to deliver the course without my further involvement.
Result	Course reduction saves 3,200 man-hours of lost productivity.

Project Focus

Client needed an instructor to deliver Unix-based computer engineering tool training on Metaphase.

Benefit	Developed working knowledge of this new Nokia system and trained 200 engineers in the United States.
Result	By learning the system quickly, the original trainer was free to go to Europe and ensure that rollout was not delayed.

Project Focus

Development and training had excess part-time instructors, high turnover, and instructor no-shows.

Actions	Restructured all recruitment, training, and evaluation steps. Developed an instructor's guideline with performance metrics and audit controls. Implemented a behavioral interview process.
Result	Reduced PT instructors from 65 to 17, eliminated no-shows, and increased retention rate to 90% (the other 10% received promotions to higher performance positions).

11/92–12/95
Overview

Cellular Operator, *Cellular Subscriber Group*   Austin, TX
Performed board repairs on digital products. Trained new personnel. Served as team leader for one year. Served on problem-solving committees to improve quality, which included implementing an ESN flex number test and a defect log into the pack computer. Revamped manufacturing line to increase production.

Overview

Training Coordinator, *Digital Cellular Factory*
Maintained training records, coordinated monthly training schedule, designed training database, and created training library.

MILITARY
1983–1991

U.S. MARINES   • Aviation Structural Mechanic   • Contamination Analyst
                • Tool Control Supervisor   • QA Inspector
Awards: Letter of commendation from Navy Secretary

EDUCATION

B.S. Business Management	University of Texas at Austin 2001 GPA 3.91
Nokia University	Training the Trainer 101
Langevin Learning Services	Instructional Design 1996
Training Needs Analysis 1996	Technical Writing 1997
Marketing Your Training 1997	Advanced Instructional Design 1998

Marine Corps Instructor School 1988

PHILLIP LANGDON'S STORY

Success Snapshot: A tech sector casualty and victim of a Nokia downsizing, an HR professional who hadn't yet finished his college degree, Phil was able to find a job with a multinational company.

Career Sweet Spot: We noted eight key projects that defined his outstanding contribution to Nokia, which enabled him to find work with a German company at a 10% salary increase.

Trouble Spot Fixed: Poor education and difficult economic situation in the tech industry.

To Use This Chart:
1. Score your resume.
2. Find Before and After RQI scores in the PYV, MCG, and CPS categories similar to your scores.
3. Strengthen your weaknesses using our tactics.

BEFORE SCORE		of 100%		Score
Category I	Prove Your Value	PYV =	13%	10 of 75
Category II	Met Corporate Goals	MCG =	0%	0 of 30
Category III	Career Progress Status	CPS =	67%	20 of 30
	Their RQI Score:		**22%**	**30 of 135**

AFTER SCORE		of 100%		Score
Category I	Prove Your Value	PYV =	100%	75 of 75
Category II	Met Corporate Goals	MCG =	100%	30 of 30
Category III	Career Progress Status	CPS =	100%	30 of 30
	Our RQI Score:		**100%**	**135 of 135**

CAREER STATS

Career Field:	Training
Old Title:	HR Instructor
New Title:	HR Instructor
Bridge or Ladder:	Lateral

IMPROVEMENT

From:	Power Puff
To:	Power Pro

KEY

Power Pro:	95% RQI	Power Pansy:	60–80% RQI
Power Prospect:	80–95% RQI	Power Puff:	Below 60% RQI

RODERICK ANDERSON

Public to Private University

CAREER HIGHLIGHTS

- Salary increase with his new resume: $18,000

- Title promotion: lateral

- Job search length: four weeks

BEFORE
RQI: 60

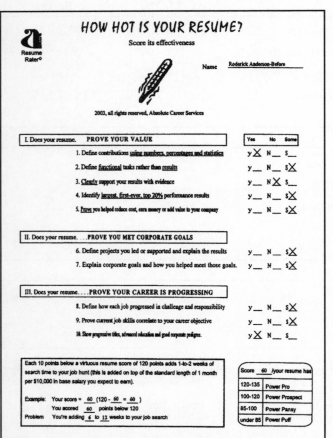

AFTER
RQI: 125

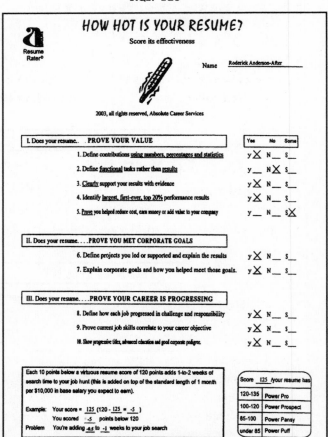

RODERICK ANDERSON
314 Pepper Ridge Lane,
Atlanta, GA 30314
404-249-3116

EDUCATIONAL BACKGROUND

Master of Science Degree in Management, 12/96
Emory University, Atlanta, GA
Concentration in Human Resource Management
3.60 GPA on 4.0 scale

Bachelor of Arts Degree in Biblical Studies, 5/78
Faulkner University, Montgomery, AL

FINANCIAL AID EXPERIENCE

7/98 to Present   Associate Director of Financial Aid
                        Mercer University

- Administer over 50 million dollars in financial assistance.
- Supervise 12 full-time staff and 17 work-study employees.
- Revamp phone system to re-direct students to their specific financial aid advisors.
- Actively participate with area feeder high schools to improve enrollment and recruitment programs.
- Serve on financial aid - bursar -admission collaborative committee.
- Improved turnaround time on processing of files by 2 months over 3 year period.
- Handle all dependency appeals and special condition students.
- Supervise satisfactory academic progress reviews of 2,500 students every year.
- Serve as liaison between financial aid office and 3 different at risk student populations.
- Supervised college work study office providing jobs to over 500 students.

4/97–5/98   Senior Assistant Director of Financial Aid
                    Georgia State University

- Handled small alpha section of undergraduate financial aid applications.
- Explained financial aid procedures to prospective incoming freshmen and transfer students and parents.
- Interfaced with admission office to create clear explanation of financial aid packages.
- Supervision of verification procedures for all selected students.

2/95–4/97 and   Director of Financial Aid
10/84–5/88   Atlanta Christian College

- Administered and coordinated awarding of over 10 million dollars in financial aid to over 2,500 students on 3 different campuses.
- Supervised 4 full time and 3 college work study students.
- Served as member of campus-wide student retention committee.
- Chaired satisfactory academic progress committee.
- Responsible for college work study program serving over 300 students.
- Set up college's first computer system to manage and track financial aid expenditures.

7/88–2/95   Assistant Director of Financial Aid
          Troy University

- Supervised 1 full time and 4 work study students.
- Awarded over 1,200 students annually with financial aid from federal and state sources.
- Set up and managed Troy's first electronic Pell Grant transmission module serving over 2,700 students.
- Managed and directed state's largest private school ISAC Monetary Award Program.

HIGHER EDUCATION EXPERIENCE

8/89–5/94
Men's Golf Coach
Troy University
Main responsibilities included instruction, team building and coordinating travel in the Southeast area.

12/99–present
Adjunct Instructor
Trinity International University
RE.A.C.H. Program
Part-time instructor in degree completion program.
Courses taught: Technology and Education Leading and Managing

PROFESSIONAL AFFILIATIONS
National Association of Student Financial Aid Administrators (NASFAA) Presenter at National
Conference, Las Vegas, Nevada 7/99
Topic: "Reward and Recognition Programs—What works and what doesn't"

RODERICK ANDERSON

314 Pepper Ridge Lane, Atlanta, GA 30314 404-249-3116

EDUCATION	M.S., H.R. Management	Emory University, Atlanta, GA 1996	
	B.A., Biblical Studies	Faulkner University, Montgomery, AL	

EXPERIENCE   **FINANCIAL AID DEPARTMENTS**

1988–present	Associate Director	Mercer University	7/98–Present
	Sr. Asst. Director	Georgia State University	4/97–5/98
	Director	Atlanta Christian College	2/95–4/97
	Assistant Director	Troy University	7/88–2/95

Role at Mercer   Manage a $1MM operating budget and lead a staff of 27 and 2 asst. directors. Serve 100–700 students a day and allocate $45 million a year.

My Goal   Support the equivalent of an 11,000-employee corporation (current enrollment) by ensuring students are led through each stage of the financial aid and scholarship process during their academic career.

Actions
Appeals   Handle all dependency appeals and special condition students.
Program Support   Liaison to 3 at-risk student populations.
Assessment   Supervise progress reviews of 2,500 students a year.
Staffing   Place 600+ student jobs a year at 70 departments •Administration •Research
          • Finance   • Science   • Accounting   • Psychology   • Library   • Retail
Teams   • Enrollment Management • Collaborative Committee • Academic Progress
Public Speaking   Present at 12 high schools to help Mercer grow enrollment.
Compliance   Respond to four audit groups (internal, private/external, federal, state).

IMPROVEMENTS
Default Prevention   **Result**: Mercer now ranks 2nd best of all Southern Urban Institutions
Applicant Processing **Result**: Reduced processing time by 42% as applications increased 10%

Role at GA State   Explained packages to students and parents. Worked with admission offices.
Compliance   Supervised verification procedures for all selected students.

Role at Atlanta
Christian   Awarded $10M in financial aid to 2,500 students on 3 campuses. Led 7 staff.
Teams   • Chair academic progress committee • Member student retention committee
Staffing   Oversaw college work study program of 300 students.

IMPROVEMENTS   Created the first information system to manage and track financial aid costs.

Role at Troy   Supervised 5 staff who awarded 1,200 students financial aid.
Funding   Packaged all NCAA Div. I athletic scholarships.
Info. Systems   Set up Troy's first electronic Pell Grant submission module.
Operations   Directed state's largest private school ISAC Monetary Award Program.

EXPERIENCE		**PROFESSIONAL DEVELOPMENT & TRAINING**
12/99–present	**Instructor**	Atlanta Christian Univ.—REACH, a degree completion program for adults.

Taught   • Technology and Communication
          • Leading and Managing
          • Applied Communication

RODERICK ANDERSON'S STORY

Success Snapshot: A director of finance at a state university who wanted to resign was able to find new employment within four weeks at a private university.

Career Sweet Spot: Hired by a prestigious private school as their financial aid director.

Trouble Spot Fixed: Proved to a private university that his work history made him the best candidate in a tough job market.

To Use This Chart:
1. Score your resume.
2. Find Before and After RQI scores in the PYV, MCG, and CPS categories similar to your scores.
3. Strengthen your weaknesses using our tactics.

BEFORE SCORE			of 100%	Score
Category I	Prove Your Value	PYV =	40%	30 of 75
Category II	Met Corporate Goals	MCG =	33%	20 of 30
Category III	Career Progress Status	CPS =	67%	20 of 30
	Their RQI Score:		**44%**	**60 of 135**

AFTER SCORE			of 100%	Score
Category I	Prove Your Value	PYV =	87%	65 of 75
Category II	Met Corporate Goals	MCG =	100%	30 of 30
Category III	Career Progress Status	CPS =	100%	30 of 30
	Our RQI Score:		**93%**	**125 of 135**

CAREER STATS

Career Field:	Financial Aid
Old Title:	Dir. Financial Aid
New Title:	Dir. Financial Aid
Bridge or Ladder:	Lateral

IMPROVEMENT

From:	Power Puff
To:	Power Prospect

KEY

Power Pro:	95% RQI	Power Pansy:	60–80% RQI
Power Prospect:	80–95% RQI	Power Puff:	Below 60% RQI

RESUME QUESTIONNAIRE

Use the following questionnaire to discover the key attributes you possess.

Last Name _____ First _____ M _____

Address _____

Telephone (_____) _____ EMAIL _____

OBJECTIVE _____

SKILLS   1. _____   2. _____   3. _____

             4. _____   5. _____   6. _____

EMPLOYMENT HISTORY: (start with most recent employer)

1. Company _____ City _____ State _____

Job Title _____

Dates Worked: From _____ To _____

Is your performance measured in any way? (i.e.; # units, dollars saved, sales made)

Break up a typical day into eight hours. List your achievements, accomplishments, or greatest challenges:

Have you worked on any corporate projects? What was the focus and the results?

Ask yourself the following questions to help you write your resume. The questions will reveal how you added value using the C.A.R. (challenge, action, result).

Challenge	List a challenge you faced in your job.
Action	What did you do to overcome the challenge?
Result	What was the result? Use Numbers, Percentages, and Quantities

Example ***She Said***		Pamela Dorfman—Executive VP of Sales & Marketing for a Jewelry Remounting Service Managed sales and service of "While you wait and watch transformation" remount services for consumers on location at jewelry retailers such as Marshall Field's, Dayton-Hudson, and Zale's stores.
We Said	**Challenge**	Optimizing thirty-five sales teams who conducted eight thousand to ten thousand remount shows per year at two thousand jewelry stores in North America.
	Action	Created an extremely efficient master schedule that tracked every show, the team's traveling, and downtime, in order to minimize conflict with peak selling seasons of our six corporate accounts and to optimize their productivity.
	Result	The new master schedule reduced per show costs from an average of $750/show to $500/show, which delivered $2.5M to the bottom line.

2. Company _____

City _____ State _____ Job Title _____

Dates Worked: From _____ To _____

Is your performance measured in any way? (i.e., # units, dollars saved, sales made)

Break up a typical day into eight hours. List your achievements, accomplishments, or greatest challenges:

Have you worked on any corporate projects? What was the focus and result?

Ask yourself the following questions to help you write your resume. The questions will reveal how you added value using the C.A.R. (challenge, action, result).

3. Company _____

City _____ State _____ Job Title _____

Dates Worked: From _____ To _____

Is your performance measured in any way? (i.e., # units, dollars saved, sales made)

Break up a typical day into eight hours. List your achievements, accomplishments, or greatest challenges:

Have you worked on any corporate projects? What was the focus and result?

Ask yourself the following questions to help you write your resume. The questions will reveal how you added value using the C.A.R. (challenge, action, result).

EDUCATION _____

Dates Attended: From _____ To _____ Major _____ Degree(s)

Career Field Examples — Who Has A Career Like Yours?

THE KEY TO THE CHART IS TO FIND CATEGORIES THAT FIT YOUR CAREER AND USE MY CLIENT'S EXAMPLE FOR YOUR RESUME.

Page	Name	Ladder	Bridge	Finance	Promotion	Sales	Marketing/Media	Recent Grad	Masters	No Degree	Blue Collar	Unemployed	One Job	Government	Executive	HR	Pharmaceutical	Fortune 500	IT/Consulting	Over 50	Teacher/Educ.	Banking	CPA	Investment	Institutional	Healthcare	Flat Career	Dead End Job	Career Plateau	GM	Retail Owner	Media	Non Profit
65	Aaron Parker	x	x		x	x	x					x					x	x													x		
69	Sam Bently	x	x								x	x	x																				
74	Jim Lambert	x	x		x	x																											
79	Richard Altman			x	x													x															
59	Jeff Conway			x																			x						x				
84	Daniel Wallace	x					x											x					x	x			x						
91	Abby Harrington	x						x						x																			
100	Elise Hanson	x	x			x																											
96	Paul Bender	x	x			x			x		x																						
105	Jennifer Johnson	x				x		x																			x						
114	Caroline Reagan			x		x		x		x							x									x							
109	April Lawrence	x					x								x			x										x					x
119	Scott Washburn	x								x				x			x	x									x			x			x
123	Eric Werner	x				x		x	x					x				x	x							x				x			x
128	Chuck Randall	x				x					x	x				x	x										x						
137	Larena Paredo				x	x	x																			x							
133	Eileen Wilkenson	x																		x					x	x							
141	Jon Hampton	x	x											x				x							x	x							
149	Nathan Rockwell	x					x		x				x					x							x								
145	Vanessa Martin	x																						x								x	x
153	Kent Bradley		x		x																			x									
177	Roderick Anderson		x	x									x					x	x	x	x												x
159	Edward Bailey	x									x		x					x	x	x						x							
165	Frederick Taylor	x	x													x	x	x	x	x						x							
171	Phillip Langdon		x							x	x					x										x						x	

ABOUT THE AUTHOR

Robert Wm. Meier began writing resumes thirteen years ago when he opened the career consulting firm Wm. Meier & Associates in 1991. Since that time he has written resumes and taught interviewing techniques and salary negotiation skills to thousands of job seekers. As a whole, his clients' net income has increased by $250 million, a princely sum that represents an average salary boost of $10,000. If you were to add up all of the accumulated wisdom in the book, the total amount would equal forty thousand years of work histories (representing an average of ten years per client), expertise that is spread across every possible employment category in the job market.

As a career-consulting pioneer, Robert Meier's methods are a radical departure from the basic approach accepted as today's standard. *The World's Greatest Resumes* explains how Mr. Meier paints original pictures of the strengths and abilities of a professional using the resume as a palette. Although unique in design and execution, these resume techniques are also effective, are easily understood, and apply to all job seekers.

Overall, Robert Meier has been covered in newspaper articles, has been interviewed by national radio programs, and is a popular public speaker at public libraries and universities. In 2002, he started the Career Corner for the Business Marketing Association, an eighty-year-old national nonprofit catering to the high-end advertising, marketing, and promotions professional. He now works out of two Chicago-based offices and is still available to consult one-on-one with clients who need a supportive expert capable of moving them from a career bottleneck into rewarding, full-time employment within or outside of their current industry.

Questions or comments for the author can be directed to coach@absolutecareer.com. You can visit his website at: www.absolutecareer.com.